Other Works by W. Phillip Keller

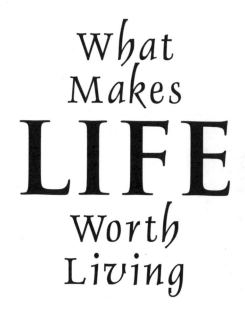

What
Makes
LIFE
Worth
Living

W. PHILLIP KELLER

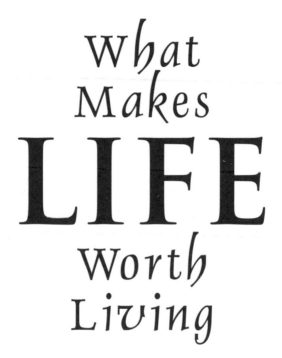

What
Makes
LIFE
Worth
Living

kregel
PUBLICATIONS

Grand Rapids, MI 49501

What Makes Life Worth Living

Copyright © 1998 by the Estate of W. Phillip Keller

Published by Kregel Publications, a division of Kregel, Inc., P.O. Box 2607, Grand Rapids, MI 49501. Kregel Publications provides trusted, biblical publications for Christian growth and service. Your comments and suggestions are valued.

For more information about Kregel Publications, visit our web site at http//:www.kregel.com.

Cover design: Frank Gutbrod
Book design: Nicholas G. Richardson

Library of Congress Cataloging-in-Publication Data
Keller, W. Phillip (Weldon Phillip), 1920–1997.
    What makes life worth living / W. Phillip Keller.
        p.   cm.
        1. Jesus Christ—Devotional literature. 2. Spiritual life—Christianity. 3. Christian life. I. Title.
BT306.5.K45   1998   248.4—dc21   97-30341
                                                                                    CIP
ISBN 0-8254-2992-7 (hardcover)

Printed in the United States of America

1 2 3 / 03 02 01 00 99 98

To Ursula,
my loyal "Cheri,"
who across the years of our marriage
has been so ready and eager for all
the adventures we have shared
in our Father's care.

Contents

Contents

Foreword

It was almost ten years ago that I prepared a foreword to Phillip Keller's compilation, *Songs of My Soul* (also a Kregel book). In that foreword I wrote:

> W. Phillip Keller has earned the accolade "a dean among Christian writers," and is, indeed, one of a vanishing breed. Every word he writes goes through the crucible of his own experience and emerges finely honed and superbly polished. He does not waste pigment as he paints pictures with words. His descriptions of his experiences in God's great out-of-doors verge on poetry—and his ongoing declaration of awe and wonder at what Jehovah God has done in creation reminds the reader of David's poetic exclamations in the Psalms.

For the thirty years or so that I knew Phillip, I marveled at his dedication and disciplined approach to the writing task—it obviously was a labor of love. Until the end of his life he meditated early and late on the Word of God and did not put pen to paper until he digested a passage and wrung unique insights from it. Walking a deserted ocean beach or climbing a lofty mountain, he pondered, ruminated, and reflected on the facets of biblical truth until he was ready to put his conclusions into words. He parroted no commentators; instead, he plowed new ground to bring a lifetime of experience to bear on a given truth.

Perhaps the secret to his exceptional way of looking at life and God is found in the foreword Phillip originally wrote for this book:

> There is a most profound appreciation for the acute awareness of Christ's presence in the project. Constantly, calmly, I have counted on Him to guide the writing by His own gracious Spirit. Morning by morning it is He who has moved upon my soul and upon my spirit to do His bidding. . . . I give hearty thanks to the Father for the courage to carry on, and for the strength to persevere to the end. Out of it may great benefit come to readers all over the earth.

I was always awestruck by Phillip's deep spiritual insights and complete commitment to the Bible as the ultimate and unique Word of God to mankind. Phillip went to be with his Lord in 1997. Now, as I contemplate his exemplary life, two passages of Scripture come to mind as "summaries" of this man of God.

First, Paul quoted God's estimation of David that "I have found [in] David son of Jesse a man after my own heart; he will do everything I want him to do" (Acts 13:22b; cf. 1 Sam. 13:14). David was not perfect, nor was Phillip Keller. But both David and Phillip had hearts for God.

Second, the writer of Hebrews said of Abel, "By faith he was commended as a righteous man, when God spoke well of his offerings. And by faith he still speaks, even though he is dead" (11:4).

God gave Phillip fifty fruitful and productive years of

writing. *What Makes Life Worth Living* is a fitting capstone to that half century of service. As Solomon wrote, "The memory of the righteous will be a blessing" (Prov. 10:7). May God continue to bless Phillip's ministry to a waiting world through this book.

Al Bryant
Grand Rapids, Michigan

Reflections of Joy

Three days ago Ursula and I celebrated my seventy-fifth birthday. We did it in quiet dignity and joyous contentment—just the two of us—good friends, wife and husband, longtime sweethearts. It was very, very special, for once again we were back in our beloved California, back in its winter warmth and sparkling sunshine.

The main purpose of our return after so long away was for me to write this book—my fiftieth book in some fifty years of steady writing. It was a book suggested first by Dennis Hillman, publisher of Kregel Publications, who has been so kind to me in recent years.

The main thought was to recount for readers, once again, some of the wondrous ways in which our Father has led me to discover the most profound purposes in life. In other words, what really matters? After all, an ordinary man who has come to truly know Christ across such a long space of time must have some deep convictions about what really counts.

Months and months of serious thought and private prayer have been given to this theme. It is indeed a challenge of the highest caliber to put down in black and white, what are the finest and most enduring values a person discovers in over three-quarters of a century of living.

Those seventy-five years have not been spent in the ease and comfort of an armchair. They have been expended in great and joyous adventures with God, my Father. They have been filled with the abundant life that Christ promised to those who follow Him. They are still replete with incredible joy and a zest known to few people who are so far down the trail. They are shared with others in deep delight and genuine gratitude.

It is no small honor to know the compelling call of Christ. To respond to His call, relinquishing all other claims to one's life, demands drastic decisions of self-abandonment to His wishes and to His supreme will. But that is the path to inner peace. It is also the way by which He reveals His noble purposes to a person. In the working out of His supreme will one finds utter fulfillment, serene satisfaction, and the potent power of Christ's own presence to prevail over adversity.

At heart, that is what this book is about. For in close company with the Master, I have learned what really matters and what does not . . . not only regarding eternal, enduring truth, but also in the tough, rough and tumble of everyday living. When people know with absolute assurance that God the Father directs their lives, then they walk humbly and quietly in His company.

This close companionship with the Most High leads to enormous joy and exhilaration in the everyday events of one's brief sojourn here. But also deep convictions are reached as to what matters most in life. The pervasive wind of God's own gracious Spirit has His own way of blowing away the dust and chaff that would otherwise settle in our souls. He consumes the hulls and husks of human folly, giving us the very living, life germ of God's eternal Word to nourish and quicken our hungry spirits.

In our Father's care there is serene satisfaction of soul.

In Christ's company there is exquisite contentment of life.

In His Spirit's gentle guidance there is power to push on!

Accepting these generous gifts is to drink deeply of Christ's own abundant life: It is joyous living!

Our return drive to California was a case in point. A very long and demanding drive of over thirteen hundred mountain miles looked formidable. Just a little over a year before, my car had been wrecked when a driver, spaced out on drugs, totally demolished it. So I wondered if such a long haul was beyond my endurance now. Quietly I entreated our Father to supply special strength for this trip and open roads over the high passes.

We left long before dawn. It was dark as dark could be, soon made even more dangerous by winter fog. Still the car ran eagerly, and to my amazement we covered the miles with ease. Then torrential rains set in—rains that caused enormous flooding across the Northwest. But the roads were open and we sped south always just on the leading edge of the storm system.

At higher elevations mixed snow and rain and sleet reduced visibility and covered the highway in dangerous slush. Just at that juncture a huge truck loaded with power equipment pulled out in front of us. We followed it steadily through the storm with absolute confidence. Thank you, Father. That first day, under such adverse weather, we had covered just over six hundred miles.

The next day was equally amazing. We had high mountain passes to traverse. Yet the roads were bare, black, and open. By midday we were out of the mountains, cruising swiftly along the Sacramento Valley in the warm sunshine of California's balmy climate. What a joyous relief!

It was a glorious way to celebrate my seventy-fifth birthday. That evening Ursula and I thoroughly relished a magnificent meal of seafood in an elegant Spanish-style restaurant. The dinner was delicious, served on white linen and adorned with white roses. The quiet country setting was splendid.

As we watched the sun settle in flaming colors beyond the coastal hills, our spirits were still and pensive in Christ's company. How tenderly He had opened the way for us. How surely He had guided us in the storms. How generously He had brought us back again to this beloved region.

The next day consisted of a glorious, gentle drive across the golden hills of this great, sprawling state by the sea. By midmorning we were driving beside the breakers. To celebrate our return we breakfasted on an open balcony where the sea waves surged on the rocks below us. What a lovely spot!

An hour later a dear, kind friend met us in a little village close to our destination. We all embraced warmly, and Ursula and I became engulfed by the awareness of being home again amid the fragrance of the eucalyptus and glorious foliage of the coast. All the way, hour by hour, an acute awareness of Christ's companionship had enriched this challenging trip. We had accomplished the drive in much less time than ever expected. Most surprising was the amazing stamina and physical strength He supplied to do the drive.

Later that afternoon we settled into our comfortable winter quarters. We had rented the suite site unseen. It, too, surpassed our fondest dreams. We accepted it with joy and gratitude as the place provided for us in which to accomplish this work.

Life is intertwined with challenges. They test our own fortitude. But even more compelling, they demonstrate to us how gracious, generous, and faithful is our Father to His children. Life with Him is truly an adventure, full of beautiful bonuses. How grateful we are!

CHAPTER ONE

Knowing God, Firsthand

The only way to actually know God, firsthand, is to let Him into all of your life! It is that simple. Yet at the same time it is also the most challenging choice anyone ever makes. For this is a profound, positive act of the will to allow another Spirit, much greater than your own, to have complete access to all of your activities.

We human beings are exceedingly reluctant to relinquish the rule of our lives to any other spirit. We are convinced that we are, to use an old expression, kings in our own castles. We insist on exerting our right to make our own decisions, even if they prove utterly self-destructive. We are sure we hold sovereign sway over our own way. We will not fully yield the control of our careers or our personal conduct to another, even if it be God Himself—our Father, our Friend, our Fellow Comrade.

There are two main misunderstandings that underlie this rigid resentment against God. First, we assume we can get along fine on our own. This is a dreadful delusion made evident by the terrible plight of so many people all over the planet. The violence of man against man, the exploitation of the poor, the awful crimes committed against innocent victims, the pain of prejudice, the ruthlessness of the rich, plus scores of other social evils cry out from the young, the poor, and the downtrodden to warn us all.

No! Men and women the world over do not get along just fine. They struggle on alone in the darkness of their despair . . . not knowing why!

The second serious misunderstanding is about God Himself. All across the long and tragic history of the human race, men and women have contrived all sorts of false and spurious gods. There have been literally thousands of deceptive deities devised by man's imagination. The worship of such false idols has led to dark delusion and utter despair that only deepen the human dilemma. So, understandably, people are very prejudiced against phony piety or any form of religious ritual that only adds burdens to their lives.

So they choose instead to ignore God. They are sure that He will somehow impose harsh restrictions on them. They imagine He is a monster. Each turns from Him to find the way alone.

Yet the joyous good news about the only true and living God is, in fact, just the opposite. Once you admit Him into your life in an open, honest, and hearty welcome, you will be astounded with delight! For you will find that this One who was so distant, so dreaded, does indeed become your loving, caring Father. You will be overwhelmed with the generosity, goodness, and compassion of the living Christ who comes to you as a Friend . . . able to deliver you from your despair. You will be amazed at the precious presence of God's Holy Spirit, who becomes your guide and guardian on life's tangled trails.

The strange inner searching of your soul will be satisfied. No human philosophy, no material achievement, no social success, no ritual or religion could ever do this. But letting the living Lord, Jesus the Christ, come into your entire being will completely re-create and reinvigorate you.

You will suddenly be acutely aware that you are entering into a brand-new dimension of living—this new life of God's own presence and power being made real, evident, and potent in you. You will know assuredly that God is very, very much alive, at work in you and active in your affairs.

Steadily, surely, you will find your entire being invaded, enfolded, filled with His overwhelming love, His serenity of spirit, His goodwill. His coming dispels doubts. His presence brings blessed peace. His power and purposes within your soul and spirit diminish your fears, giving sure direction to your days.

Suddenly in the midst of a frantic world, caught up in the cross fire of chaos and confusion, you discover you have rest and restoration in Him. An aura of deep contentment begins to pervade your person, simply because you are relinquishing control of all your concerns to God Himself, who alone knows and understands all your perplexities and has all the solutions.

Remarkable as it seems, you will know what it means to be set free from all the fears, the folly, and the frustrations of your former life. The empty, pointless futility of your feverish struggles to get ahead will be replaced with a calm confidence in His care.

You can relax in your Father's compassion.

You can trust in Christ's companionship.

You can calmly obey and follow the gentle guidance of His gracious Spirit.

This is to truly know the living Lord God firsthand. He is no longer some distant deity. He is here with you, never to leave you. And so all is well!

The intense, intimate relationship with the living God, if allowed to flourish, changes and re-creates us completely.

The transformation first begins within the human spirit, at the very center of our being. Not only does a keen awareness steal into our inner consciousness that we are in the very presence of God—the Supreme Eternal Spirit, who is utterly righteous—but He also makes us acutely conscious of our own unrighteousness.

In our profound remorse we repent of our sins, we turn from our own wicked ways, and in deep contrition cast ourselves upon His amazing mercy and grace. In the intense brightness of His own beautiful character, we see ourselves as we really are—defiled. So in desperate need of forgiveness and acceptance we come to Him to be made whole within.

Never, never has He turned anyone away who seeks Him in sincerity. The great, insatiable, inner hunger of our spirits to be fully satisfied is fully met. The burning thirst of soul for spiritual sustenance from the refreshing springs of the Savior's own life is assuaged. New life, supernatural life, the abundant life of the living Christ is imparted to the person who in desperation turns from the old, barren, bleak ways of the world to keep company with Christ.

Living this new life is a question of choices. Day by day in calm compliance with His wishes I must choose to deny my old selfish, self-centered desires in order to do His will. It is by the power of His presence at work within my soul and spirit that He sets me free from my former folly and futility to follow Him in surety and strength. This is to walk with God in goodwill.

Stirred, moved, made subject to His sublime and noble purposes, my little life takes on enormous meaning. There breaks over my inner consciousness the realization that I really do count. Why? Because I am now a child of God, enfolded in my Father's care. Because I discover Christ Himself is both my Savior and my special Friend. Because I sense and know firsthand what it is to be guided and inspired by His gracious Spirit. All in all, life with God becomes a joyous adventure.

There is nothing, nothing else that matters more.

This is the supreme secret to life.

This is to know God.

From this gentle but glorious companionship there springs up within my spirit an outpouring of love and loyalty to Him in immeasurable proportions. I want to please Him. I long to live with Him in dignity and honor. I am prepared to trust Him fully for all of my life in all of my activities. I am His! Now, too, He is mine.

Human language is strained here to fully explain the spiritual depths of this exchange of life between God and man. It is at the same time so serene, so simple, yet in its own manner so sublime and so supernatural. God's gracious Spirit declares it to be the supreme secret, the marvelous mystery between God our Father and His children—Christ in you!

Changing you!

Re-creating you!

Conforming your character to His own.

This is what is meant by letting Him into your life, day by day, in every way, in all of your activities.

Life with God is not confined to just the realm of the person's spirit. It finds ever increasing expression in the soul of man, in his contact with others, in the constant interaction with the circumstances of our society and our culture.

The re-created individual very soon discovers that the invasion of His Spirit makes a powerful impact on the soul. The coming of Christ into my life alters my inner attitudes and the expression of my emotions. This is inevitable. His compassion, His care for others, His charity toward the unfortunate becomes a part—an important part—of my makeup.

Bit by bit, step-by-step, year by year an inexorable transformation takes place in my entire thought life. By Christ's presence within, and through the impact of His Word on my mind, my whole value system is reformed. I begin to clearly see the world and all its wrong views in the bright light of God's wisdom and eternal truth.

For the first time Christ enables me to discover that I was deceived by the false values, the utter folly, and the terrible futility of a worldly society. I understand the inherent corruption of our crass civilization.

Because of these titanic transformations in my thinking, my priorities are put into proper order. Pride is pulverized. My strong will and stubborn soul submit in sincerity to God's gracious goodwill. He then empowers me to go out calmly day by day, amid all the confusion around me, and choose quietly in faith and confidence to do His bidding.

There is nothing sensational or even spectacular about this ongoing change. It is the quiet impact of Christ's presence upon my character and my conduct from hour to hour. Ten thousand tiny deliberate decisions eventually lead to enormous events that God undergirds, simply because He has found a soul open and available to His entrance. Sad to say, there are so very few who choose to walk with Him in this humble, honest companionship.

But for those who do, there are joyous delights of magnificent meaning. This is not to say life instantly becomes "a bowl of cherries," but it does mean that despite every adversity, no matter how much suffering, He is here! He is with me to help and to heal! So all is in order.

As a result, for the person who truly knows God firsthand, there are pleasures forevermore in His presence. There is a sparkle in the eyes. There is a smile on the face. There is a spring in the step, even into old age. There is a cheerful outlook on a world all awry. There is the bright assurance that our Father is still very much at work behind all the dark clouds of this century. There is the bright hope of heaven and the sure knowledge of sharing in His life forever and forever!

In the interim He calls us to be ever loyal to Him in bringing His love to the lost, His own life to those in death, His light and freedom to those struggling in the darkness of their despair. This is what matters most! It is a noble honor to have a small part in His glorious purposes for all of us.

CHAPTER TWO

The Honor of Honest Work

When Christ lived and moved and ministered among us in the person of Jesus of Nazareth, He made His short sojourn here one of steady service. During His formative years and all through His youth and early manhood He worked diligently at His trade as a carpenter and builder. He became well-known in Nazareth as "the carpenter," skilled, honest, reliable, and fair in His fees.

He worked steadily to support not only Himself but also His siblings, for He was the firstborn son in the family. Later He had His widowed mother, Mary, to care for as well. All of this humble labor for some sixteen years of His life was not something to be dismissed.

For when He finally set down the tools of His private trade in order to begin a more public service, He was complemented openly by the Most High. At Christ's baptism in the Jordan River by John the Baptist, a flaming prophet from the desert, His Father declared audibly from on high, "You are my beloved Son, in whom I am well pleased!"

So it is apparent that from our Father's perspective, any honest work done with dignity is noble, honorable, and well pleasing to God. This is most important to know!

Later in His very public life Christ worked constantly to serve others. He insisted He came to serve. Tremendous demands were made on Him to heal the sick, to feed the hungry, to hearten the downtrodden, to help those in sorrow, to rescue and save lost people, to teach others truth.

And all of it was heavy, hard, honest work. He always called this service "my Father's work." He insisted, in plain terms, "My Father works—and I work!" The work He did was His Father's will.

This is a profound perception! It elevates any task entrusted to us by God our Father to a lofty level. It means that any labor performed with love and humility in cooperation with Christ, no matter how simple or menial, can be a supreme service of great honor. It is a noble enterprise in which both God and man are jointly engaged—for His honor and for our good.

This view of our work brings gentle dignity into the drabness and drudgery of any day—no matter what its demands.

A person may sweep streets and sing in his soul.

A mother may care for tiny tots or tough teenagers and see it as an honorable and high calling.

An intern may bathe the open, suppurating sores of lepers and do so having a sparkle in the eye.

Any layperson can labor at the most menial job and bring to it the dignity of work well done and the gift of benediction for laboring as Christ's servant.

As a simple, forthright reminder to myself of what true work in company with Christ really means, I have a marker in the book of my daily devotions that states:

> Before you cry in your distress, always bless the Lord first for His faithfulness to you in life. Then your simple tasks, done faithfully with Him each day, become lovely mosaics, laid down in the humble pavement of your private walk with Him.

23

The faithful work of which I speak is not a form of tedious toil; rather it is a labor of love. Though it may be ordinary work—pruning a rosebush, baking bread, visiting a forlorn friend, tending a little tot—each task can carry something of joy. We can, if we so choose, discover deep delight in work well done with a smile on our faces and laughter on our lips.

For me as a man, work—any work, heavy work, hard work, steady work—has been hearty work. It has been happy work. And it matters most that it be honest work, for Christ and I are engaged in the endeavor as a team.

So very often I have turned to Him who is at my side and requested the skill, the stamina, and the serenity to push the job through with goodwill as well as with good success. He does not defraud me. I gladly accepted the challenge because the work becomes a real adventure with Him.

Having His guidance in my work has been a most important part of my whole life, even during the willful years of my youth when I did not always walk with God as I do now. In His generosity He shared in my enterprises and gave me energy to go on. In every field of endeavor He was my alongside Friend. In the years of scientific study and research, in acting as an agricultural consultant, in developing my own magnificent ranches, in resource studies throughout the world, in production of wildlife films and photographs, in writing some fifty books across fifty years, in addressing thousands of churches everywhere—in all of these activities there has been a compelling sense of my Father, God Himself, active and at work in my affairs. It has been His presence, His power, His peace that assures my soul He is here to help, to guide, to inspire. I do not perform the work at hand on my own. Even in the sequence in which the tasks of the day are tackled, I am sensitive and open to His divine direction.

His presence adds a bright aura of expectancy and beautiful bonuses to the day. It is quite remarkable to sense and know that He is arranging the day's events in such detail. With this sublime stimulus of spirit I can work well. Work—any kind of work—then becomes a joy, not just a job. The task becomes a joint effort carried out calmly but with deep contentment in work well done, on time, with excellence.

After all, my Father's name, honor, and respect are at stake in the work I do. The whole world watches my job performance. Sad to say, and it needs to be said emphatically, far too often Christians are seen cutting corners, loafing on the job, being careless about quality and irresponsible in their prior commitments.

Such laxity brings enormous discredit to Christ. It often explains why secular people despise Christians. It underlies the current contempt for the church. It fuels skepticism toward those who follow the Master.

But by the same measure, Christians who do noble, honest, excellent work will gain the attention of the ungodly. Try it, and see what God will do!

After all, one thing that matters most in life is the way in which we discharge our duties. Work is not a wicked word! It is a noble honor given to each of us and helps to make our world a more congenial environment not only for the human race, but for all creatures great and small. Our Lord God loves them all.

We often overlook the great fundamental fact that a person's work represents in practical, enduring terms what he or she considers to be important. In subsequent chapters, I will explore in depth other facets that truly matter in life. But it remains true that an individual's work represents a significant contribution to the world in which we all live.

We sometimes forget that if an individual, through the expenditure of energy, time, and thought, creates something of worth, it remains as an enduring reminder of a life well spent. This is especially true if the duties have been performed in honesty, kindness, and care for others.

Christ Himself made much of work as service. He never suggested we should all be geniuses or specially gifted people who could produce masterpieces. But He did declare that even the most lowly deed done in His honor to help another was, if done with noble motives, really done to Him and for Him.

He insisted this sort of special, sublime service could be as uncomplicated as giving a thirsty person a cup of cool water or taking the time to walk a second mile with someone sad or forlorn. It could be freeing an ox mired in the mud.

My own candid view is that Christ never intended us to "strut our stuff" in proud self-promotion. He does not call us to some special, sophisticated sort of man-exalted ministry. Rather He calls us to simply follow Him in lowly, humble service to a suffering, sin-driven society shot through with sorrow.

Just recently my wife and I were taken to a special Christmas concert put on by one of the elite Christian colleges of the country. I went in joyous expectation of hearing great hymns and grand music that would lift up our spirits in exultation of Christ our King. Instead, the staff of the music department had arranged a program of complicated pieces that proudly showed off their own skills. The music was so loud, so discordant, so avant-garde that it was almost impossible to understand.

The overall impression was nothing more than a proud, pathetic performance that pandered to the conductor's ego, very much like a nightclub show. Thus a splendid chance to offer royal, loyal honor and service to our Savior had been missed completely. I came home saddened in soul.

The work we do must always be seen as for, and with, God because we are both engaged in the enterprise. The work must be a credit, both to Him and to us. After all, His name, His honor, His reputation are at stake in it and in us. So our service is one of divine dignity.

If He is well pleased with the work He will honor it in His own gracious way. It will endure, even long after we have passed from the scene. He will use it to touch, bless, and enrich others whom we will never ever meet or see. He can make our simple service a sublime benediction.

This dimension of doing the Master's bidding brings powerful purpose and superb direction into all of life. It adds meaning to the most menial and mundane tasks we tackle. Our work is no longer a monotonous drag, a forlorn drudgery, or a dehumanizing endeavor. Rather, it becomes a noble service to the Most High and to others whom He wishes to touch through us.

I have observed throughout a long life of hard work that our Father arranges His own unique and lovely rewards for work well done in good cheer. He has His gentle way of surprising those who are faithful servants with beautiful bonuses of His own design. He always honors those who in their work honor Him. Not necessarily with human accolades or public recognition, but in profound inner contentment and an acute awareness that He keeps all the accounts. In due course He sees to it that the last shall be first, and the least shall be the greatest.

God has the ultimate rewards for work well done. In the end He decides how the honors are awarded. All He asks of me is to be steadfast and loyal to Him wherever He places me in His service.

It is in this sure knowledge that work is an honor. When done in honesty and to the best of my ability it can be a delight. Because He, too, is active in it with me, it carries great dignity, worth, and inspiration!

Then I can serve with a smile.

Then I can whistle while I work.

Then I can see adventure in my activities with Him.
Then I can feel fulfilled with joy.
Then I can follow Christ in quiet contentment—
Anywhere!

CHAPTER THREE

Do What You Do Best —and Love It!

One of the awful tragedies of human history consists of the innumerable lives spent, wasted, thrown to the winds in merely existing. This has been a large part of the human problem on the planet. I have seen such waste in its most stark and dark dimensions in various countries all over the earth. It makes no difference whether it is the highly-paid executive trapped in his treadmill job on the twentieth floor of a shining skyscraper in New York, or an African peasant clad only in a loincloth and trapped on his tiny plot of waste ground under the burning sun.

Millions upon millions of people spend their entire existence on earth in deadening drudgery. They are yoked to a treadmill of tedium. Life for multitudes is meaningless. Even the wages earned or money received is a mockery, for it is the very thing that binds them into endless bondage and dark skepticism.

This is not an easy chapter to write. I know firsthand what it is to be caught in the awful, soul-destroying tangle of pointless toil. I endured much at the hands of tough taskmasters in my youth. The longer I labored with aching back, screaming muscles, and tired tendons, the more my will was set to break free from such bondage.

I was determined I would discover what I could do best—what I could do well with a natural, joyous instinct—work that I loved and relished. For early in my working years, I learned that the man who loves what he is doing can overcome huge obstacles. Reverses and setbacks are no longer calamities, but become challenges to be overcome and stepping stones to the future.

What has just been written is of paramount importance for God's person. A handsome paycheck, prestige, even power and influence garnered only for one's own ends are not reason enough to pursue a certain career or enter a chosen profession.

There are two other considerations that matter more! First, is this in fact the work God my Father wishes me to do?

Second, has He endowed me with the special abilities to do it well, with joy?

It is utterly astonishing to see how many people really have missed the mark in life. They have not found the high and noble calling for which God Himself equipped them. Too often they are square pegs trying to fit in round holes. They simply do not fit! And the end result is cruel frustration or empty ennui.

Many, many young people come to me asking earnestly what to do with their lives. The choice of a career is a most serious matter! It matters so much whether or not one enjoys one's work. My reply is always the same: Do what you can do best, find out what you love eagerly to do, then fling yourself wholeheartedly into the endeavor. Trust Christ to direct your decisions.

This does not mean that life will always be smooth sailing over calm waters. It will not! It never is for anyone.

There will be storms. There will be dark days. There will be testing situations and confrontations with tough people.

But the great secret in the storms is that you are not in this wind-whipped gale all on your own. You can sense the powerful presence of the Master with you. He is beside you to guide, encourage, and keep you on course. So you can carry on calmly. You can overcome. You can succeed.

Additionally, it should be known that anyone who does excellent work with gracious goodwill is going to be well rewarded in several ways. First and foremost, there seeps into one's own spirit an acute awareness that the task has been accomplished with finesse. It is a joint project between God and man. Such a sensation brings dignity, honor, and solid satisfaction into life.

Secondly, such work always attracts attention. As the old truism put it so well, "If a man builds a better mousetrap or writes a better book, even though he lives in the woods, the world will beat a path to his door." That is absolutely so!

During the years that I wrote some of my books in tiny cabins tucked away in remote mountain valleys of British Columbia, editors and publishers went to great pains to track me down. In those rough, tough days they would have to sit by an open fire and share a cup of strong tea boiled from water drawn out of a mountain spring.

No, we don't need Madison Avenue advertising or the hype of Hollywood with all its tarnished tinsel to prove our work is worthy of acclaim. Our Father sees to that when the work is well pleasing to Him.

The sorry truth is that too often workers try to impress their contemporaries rather than being content just to work well in company with Christ Himself. He honors those who humbly honor Him. That is what matters most!

Thirdly, He has a wondrous way of providing for those who put His interests first in their endeavors. He cares for them as they carry on quietly. He inspires them in their efforts. He pours out His bounties and His benefits on the individual who works in integrity.

A person's work, no matter what it is, should stand on its own merit. If it is to endure it must be of honest, noble, intrinsic worth. As God's child I do not cut corners, turn out trash, or pass off halfhearted endeavors hoping high-pressure publicity can make up for the obvious deficiencies.

That may be the way contemporary society does it, but it is not the way a godly person does it.

Let me say it again. God's name, God's reputation, God's esteem is at stake in my work in the world. So, I dare not do a halfhearted job. It must be done well and it must be done with goodwill. Hospice

Not only is my Father's honor to be upheld in all of my endeavors but, as His man, so also must my own. This applies whether my work is sweeping the sidewalk or speaking to an audience of a thousand souls. My life is an open document being read with cynical scrutiny by a skeptical society.

If the life and love and labor of the living Christ is to be seen at all in our sin-sotted world, it must be seen in the solid, sincere work I accomplish in His energy. It is not enough for God's people to indulge in endless sentiments and sweet talk about perishing people. God calls us to actually do some solid good work in this weary old world. One of the finest accolades ever bestowed on Christ was, "He went about doing good"!

In the end, a man's work is in essence the expression of a man's character. Jesus Himself declared, "A good tree produces good fruit. An evil tree produces inferior fruit. You do not gather figs from wild thistles. By their fruit you know what a man's character is."

I shall never forget a memorable morning that illustrates this principle. For years I had worked diligently to produce a set of documentary films showing the life habits of the major wildlife species in the Northern Rockies. When the project was completed it was submitted to the Canadian Broadcasting Corporation.

They were most interested in broadcasting the series from coast to coast. However, they made it clear to me that government policy would not permit me, as an ardent Christian, to promulgate my personal beliefs in God on this national broadcast.

In due course the films were shown to enthralled audiences. So great was the popular demand that they were broadcast four times. Letters came to me from all across the country expressing thanks for the inspiration in the work and the superb beauty of the production.

But most moving was the morning I left the studios for the last time. The chief director called me into his office and made this simple comment: "We get all sorts of sordid types coming through these studios. But your coming has been a fresh wind of uplift for all of us!"

It was enough! The work itself had spoken louder and more clearly than any comments I might have made about my personal beliefs in God. This is true, too, for the enduring legacy left behind by anyone who has done great, noble, honest work.

I feel an upsurge of profound appreciation to those who diligently labor and, inspired by the Most High, give us great music and art, great books and architecture, great parks, great health, great discoveries, great highways, or great inspiration of any sort.

Each of us in our own humble endeavors can make a noble and beautiful contribution to our generation. No matter how simple our service to the Master, and to others, it can be offered with a smile and in a spirit of generous goodwill. The prospect of making a difference for God gives an edge of excitement to even the most ordinary experiences.

It dispels the drudgery. It injects light and laughter and love into our work in the world.

In my worn, leather wallet is a faded slip of paper. On it are inscribed these simple, yet profound, thoughts first penned by Ralph Waldo Emerson (1803–1882):

> To laugh often and love much; to win the respect of intelligent persons and the affection of children; to earn the approbation of honest citizens and endure the betrayal of false friends; to appreciate beauty; to find the best in others; to give of one's self; to leave the world a bit better, whether by a healthy child, a garden patch or a redeemed social condition; to have played and laughed with enthusiasm and sung with exultation; to know even one life has breathed easier because you have lived— this is to have succeeded!

This in truth is a wholesome view of what matters most.

We live and work and play in a spirit of godliness, not to impress others or to gain merit with God our Father. We do it out of a deep, compelling sense of gratitude and thanks for all of His generosity and grace to us. Put simply but sharply, I love to work this way because He first loved me this way! That is my motive.

Most definitely yes! The ordinary work a person performs in dignity and decency can be used in the most extraordinary ways by Christ to draw onlookers to Himself. For after all He is the One who is at work in those of us who share life with Him. So it follows that our labor with Him dissipates the boredom or tedium that might otherwise dog our days. Instead, our work can be an inspiration to ourselves and to those we serve. HOSPICE

Recently I received a card from a person who had been in our Bible studies. It was sent to commemorate my seventy-fifth birthday. It was one of the finest tributes to a teacher I have ever received. It moved me mightily. In eloquent language, it stated what I have been trying to express in this chapter. Allow me to share it with you. Then you too can understand why honest work can count for God when you love doing it and truly care about doing it well.

To a teacher who cared:

> Because you care to find a way
>> To show God's love all through the day,
> Your students sensed, your students heard
>> The message deeper than the word.
> Compassion, justice, strength, speak well
>> Of God! Yes, there are ways to tell
> Of faith which permeates you so.
>> The Holy Spirit's inner glow
> Speaks more than you will ever know,
>> Because you cared!

That is to love one's work in Christ!

CHAPTER FOUR

Laughter—Great Medicine and Mirth

Show me the person who can laugh in the face of adversity and reverses, and I will show you the man or woman who can whip the whims of life. They will rise up in mirth and take their mountains of hard knocks with a grin and a chuckle.

Genuine, hearty laughter is one of the greatest gifts imparted to us by our Father. It has the amazing power to diminish our pain, lift our souls in joyous good cheer, while providing bright hope for the unknown days ahead.

For me joyous laughter is in actual fact what God's gracious Spirit calls "the oil of gladness." It is the rich, smooth, gentle, warmhearted goodwill that reduces the rub of frustration and friction between people, and between people and the pressures of life's daily demands.

Learning to laugh in trouble, at trouble, and over trouble is one of the supreme secrets to serenity amid stress. It is an element in our human behavior that matters most! It makes a world of difference in how much wear and tear we suffer.

Please do not misunderstand me. I am not speaking

about the empty, laughing doubt of cynicism, which grows increasingly common in our culture. Nor am I referring to the snide sarcasm and empty jests that heap scorn on a world all awry. Those are sad expressions of dark humor that erupt out of the deep despair of skeptical people.

But I am thinking of those hardy souls who refuse to feel sorry for themselves; who are determined to find some fun in life even when things appear to go wrong; who can set their soul free to smile and laugh even in their tears.

Honest, deep, sincere laughter is, for God's person, an expression of great joy. It is a way of giving vent to the deep inner joy that comes from truly knowing God as the loving Father who cares for us. Inherent in the very act of laughing there lies a profound declaration that our confidence is in Christ our beloved Friend. And, even when the choices we must make seem unpleasant and life's trail is entangled with trouble, we can laugh in the situation because God's own gracious Spirit is present to guide us, to lead us out in joy.

But the responsibility for radiant and lighthearted goodwill as God's children rests with us. Allow me to put it another way.

Will I choose to look for the silver lining?

Will I choose to look into Christ's face today?

Will I choose to look for my Father's hand at work behind the scenes?

If I do this deliberately, quietly, in calm confidence that He is able to bring something of benefit out of the dark days, I shall learn to laugh in pure joy at adversity. This does not mean that I am a silly soul who does not take my spiritual walk with God seriously. Quite the opposite. It is because I see Him active and at work wherever He leads me that life is shot through with shafts of light and love and laughter. My laughter, therefore, is not to mask dark tragedy; it is a triumph over trouble.

All of us have our share of trouble. There simply are no exceptions. Christ Himself declared that formidable fact. The deep question is, How will I take trouble? In dismay or in thanks?

Recently the stirring strains of Handel's *Messiah* moved me to the depths of my spirit. Again and again the majestic oratorio reminds us that Christ Himself was a Man of Sorrows and acquainted with grief. He was despised and rejected of men. He was accused and He was abused relentlessly, falsely, cruelly. Yet He triumphed not only in His death but also in His daily life.

Unshakable evidence of this bright side to His behavior lay in the great appeal of His person to common people, to the outcasts of society, and to the tiny tots who came tumbling after Him. There was sunshine, gladness, joy, and goodwill in Him that found easy rapprochement with the down-and-outers of His day. It was His way of showing His buoyant love to a broken, desperate world.

His adversaries and accusers charged Him with being "a friend to publicans and sinners." Utterly amazing! Neither prostitutes, schemers, nor starry-eyed youngsters are drawn to those who are dour or sour in their disposition. No, indeed. Christ came among us then as He comes into our lives today—bubbling over with goodwill and good cheer. And this joy finds full expression in soft chuckles, hearty laughs, and broad smiles. That really matters most!

Again and again He spoke these glad and joyous words to the broken and battered ones He met: "Be of good cheer." "Be of good cheer." "Be of good cheer." And that is utterly impossible to do on our own.

Thus, whenever I encounter a dark moody person, dour in demeanor, always drab and distraught, I have to wonder if ever they truly met the Master. For He always, always gives us the joy of His own life to replace the dreadful, dry ashes of our old adversity. Indeed He gives us beauty for ashes.

In all of this glad activity we discover a remarkable secret that our Father uses again and again to draw others, through us, to Him: it is our ability to laugh. I do not know of any other element in life that can build a bridge of trust, goodwill, and glad-hearted mirth to other men and women. It can break down barriers and cross chasms of stark cynicism quicker than anything else in all this tired old world with its fear, suspicion, and ennui.

When in sincerity, honesty, and kindness we bring smiles and fun and good cheer into our human encounters, a bridge has been built over which our love, compassion, and care can pass to others. They will soon see that we are not stiff, starchy "saints"; we are not somber, dull "do-gooders"; we are not just "holy Joes." They will see we are joyous, jolly, contented people in whom something of the very life of Jesus Christ is very evident.

This is something that matters most for each of us.

Some of the most memorable moments in all of my life have been those when I have been able to gain entrance to a closed soul and shut mind with a touch of mirth and the honest tenderness of true compassion. In an amazing manner most people can quickly detect the difference between empty, silly jests and genuine gestures of good cheer. They will readily respond to godly goodwill and gentle serenity.

Just recently I had a beautiful demonstration of this principle at work. I had gone for a long, pleasant hike along the empty beach early in the morning. When I returned it was to find that a long-haired, sun-browned "beach boy" had parked his beach buggy near my truck. He had a seagoing kayak with him. He was preparing to launch it into the rough, tumbling breakers kicked up by the overnight storm.

I could have just passed him by with a simple nod. Instead I chose to stop and spend a few precious moments with this tall, heavily muscled man—a total stranger. At first he taunted me a bit for being so brash as to take a dip in the rough water at this early hour.

My instant reply was to laugh heartily. Then I quietly remarked to him that it was true, at seventy-five years of age, the old heart found it challenging to keep my body warm in such chilly winter conditions. I was not a young buck anymore, able to stand long exposure to winter weather.

Both of us had a hearty laugh over this. Then I told him of my own private hope to one day own a sturdy kayak. In a matter of minutes we were into a profound discussion of the stillness, serenity, and inspiration one could find in quiet waters beyond the breakers, of the gentle solitude on remote lakes, of the need to be alone.

Before we parted, a bridge of confidence, trust, and goodwill had been built between us. He said he came there often and welcomed me to use his kayak. When he pulled away it was with a hearty shout of good cheer and a friendly wave of goodwill. In our next encounter it would be an honor and joy to speak to him of Christ.

Joyous, loving laughter that springs up spontaneously from the depths of a sincere spirit, right with God and man, is a purifying element in everyday life. Like pure, sparkling, mountain springwater it has the power to cleanse all it touches. It has the wondrous potency to bring refreshment, healing, and life itself to those who drink deeply of its delight.

Laughter of this sort contributes much to contentment in difficult times and challenging circumstances. It is probably the most important gift to us from our Father and helps us keep a sense of proportion in our outlook. We do not take the slings and stones of adversity too seriously. Instead we rejoice buoyantly in the greatness and goodness of Jesus Christ, our constant Friend and Savior, who can set us free from every fear, every sin of every sort.

The very first compelling command from on high, given to us mortals about this glorious Emancipator was, "Thou shalt call his name Jesus: for he shall save his people from their sins" (Matt. 1:21 KJV).

Our sins are of every sort. They come in many colors. They are not just vice or degradation but also despair, doubts, hot tempers, angry words that wound, impatience in petty matters, wrong attitudes in adversity, lack of love in life. Only Christ can set us free from the curse of these destructive emotions and give us His joyous good cheer—because He is here to save!

It is His presence;
It is His power;
It is His peace;
It is His person;
It is His pardon;
It is His purity;
It is His preservation that are my portion!

Therein lies the supreme secret to a spiritual life of enormous strength and calm assurance: We must be centered in Christ. We can laugh with genuine goodwill even when the world is all awry. For the secret fountain of upwelling joy is found in the inner, indwelling Person of the living Christ. Tapping into the source is to rejoice in the Lord. It is to know firsthand the healing, wholesome life of God our Father flowing to us, in us, through us to touch the thirsty ones around us. His gracious Spirit brings the soothing balm of Gilead to a suffering world through the secret supply of gladness He shares with us.

For me, as an ordinary man upon the road of all pilgrims who pass through the struggles we all share in common, laughter is one of the most noble gifts from God I can bestow on those I meet on life's painful path. It really matters!

Laughing heartily not only heals my mind, my emotions, my will, my consciousness of Christ, my conscience, my inmost spirit, my entire physical body, but also it helps to heal the bruises and wounds of a world gone wrong. It releases the very life of Christ into any crisis, for with Him there are no crises. He knows full well all the future, and smiles at the apparent calamity that I may find so threatening.

By all of what has been said here, I do not imply God's child should be given to silly behavior or foolish, empty jesting. Only for those who do not know Christ firsthand is life a bad joke. But for those of us who walk with Him in close companionship and intimate communion, life is shot through with light, laughter, love, and buoyant good cheer. All because He is here!

CHAPTER FIVE

Others—Caring, Giving, Encouraging

It is the glorious dawn of the first day of 1996. Red streamers of brilliant clouds tinted by the rising sun illuminate the eastern sky. Silhouetted against this magnificent backdrop of splendor stand tall palms and sturdy pines etched in black against the sunrise. In silent wonder I watch and wait and whisper:

Oh living Lord, Jesus Christ—my friend!
Oh loving God, my dear Father!
Oh gracious Holy Spirit, my constant guide!
In this year of 1996, with your joy, your love, your Laughter I quietly resolve to try and touch someone in care each day of this year.

It is the only new year's resolution I made in 1996. Yet in essence it embraces much of what really matters most! Reaching lost souls is actually what Christ calls us to do. The very core of His coming to us at all in human guise has always been twofold: to save us from the sinister shackles of our sins, and to reveal to us the true life and character of our caring, heavenly Father!

When by our own implicit and sincere invitation we invite Him to enter our own lives as Heaven's Royalty, He then asks us to live as He does. He invites us to share actively and wholeheartedly in caring for others, in giving to others, in encouraging others. This is the essential center of His own generous, gracious, godly character. And He expects it to be ours, too, as He gently lives out His life in us day by day.

We cannot claim to be Christian men and women and then not care for others.

By caring I do not refer to the popular programs and special strategies so often established by church leaders, which try to impact society, or the never-ending efforts by various agencies to reach out to the lost and perishing. They have their place, and they do perform a worthwhile role. I have shared in them. But in this chapter I am dealing with the firsthand, personal, often private, interaction one person has with another. Because if our generation is to get a glimpse of God in this present era, they must first detect something of His character in me . . . in you!

There is a remarkable, growing appetite in our people for spiritual reality. For too long, for far too long, God has been ignored, spurned, and even despised by the so-called intelligentsia of the Western world. They have foisted their worldly wisdom upon unsuspecting humankind. The end result is the endless confusion and empty ennui of the masses. No wonder that in their dark despair they yearn for something better—for life with supernatural serenity and gentle purpose to it.

So I state without apology that their first taste of eternal truth, of divine delight in life, of pulsing purpose to their days, comes from firsthand contact with God's people. That first encounter may be as brief as a warm smile, an understanding look, a gentle remark of genuine goodwill, a touch on the shoulder, a bit of joyous laughter, a simple gesture of genuine generosity to a stranger, the thoughtfulness to stop a few moments and listen intently to what the other person tells me.

Just a while ago I met some new neighbors who came from South Africa. The gentleman, now very elderly, had been the mayor of Cape Town, that magnificent city at the Cape of Good Hope.

During our opening conversation both of them expressed a great longing for their native land. In fact, they were homesick. One way they expressed their deep yearning was to say they never saw lamb meat in the local butcher shops. Lamb was one of their favorite dishes, now apparently denied them in this faraway place.

I have always been very fond of lamb myself. No matter where we live, Ursula and I manage to find this delicious meat. This locale was no exception, and so a few days later we saw some choice lamb chops on sale. I selected the best cuts and carried them off in glee.

Without any advance notice, I simply showed up at our neighbor's door, lamb chops in hand, and bestowed this bounty on them with a grin. Never, ever, will I forget the radiant smiles that swept across their faces. They showed pure, unabashed delight!

They threw wide open the door to their home—and to their hearts. They welcomed me in with the warmest hospitality and sincere gratitude. Those few lamb chops given with grace and goodwill achieved more in five minutes than months of protracted preaching could ever accomplish.

All so simple, so sincere, so satisfying.

Nothing pious or pretentious. Just sharing a bit of laughter, joy, and love!

In our pilgrimage through life it is inevitable that, unless we live very cloistered, self-centered lives, our daily paths will cross the trails of others. These encounters are not chance meetings or merely random events. Rather, they are opportunities for us to quietly do something beautiful for our Father and for those strangers He sends to us.

This element of life has always excited me. Not that I am a gregarious person with a natural affinity for people. Quite the opposite. Still, I often sense that certain people have been sent to me by my Master. They may be angels in disguise sent to aid and assist me on my way. Or they are perhaps seeking souls whom Christ expects me to introduce to Him without fanfare or pious pretense.

As we well know, our lives as God's people are under the most intense scrutiny from a watching world. Astonishing as it may sound, they not only observe what we *do*, but they scrutinize what kind of people we *are*. They may scoff at our devotion to Christ, yet they expect us to be distinct and different in our deportment toward them.

Perhaps the single most important criteria that they use to measure us by is the simple, burning question: Does this person really care about me for my own sake? Are they honestly interested?

Human beings have an incredible capacity deep within their souls to detect pretence or empty playacting. They can sense the phony show! Yet they respond to genuine concern and honest goodwill in the same way flowers open to the sun.

Therefore I have come to realize how very important it is to treat others with respect, dignity, good cheer, and gratitude. A warm smile, a firm handshake, a caring touch on the shoulder, a sincere compliment, a lighthearted bit of humor, a genuine expression of encouragement—each can ignite a sense of worth and hope in the day for another pilgrim on the path of life.

I, for one, have grown weary of the intense hype and Hollywood glitz that attends so many Christian endeavors to reach perishing people. It is as if high-powered preaching, glamorous musicians screaming into their microphones, and gigantic conventions with highly paid performers could somehow convince our generation to seek God.

Perhaps the path I prefer seems far too simple, too ordinary, too slow to attract and astonish our crude, crass culture. But it is the path of humility, compassion, and profound love that Christ Himself trod during His short sojourn among us in human guise two thousand years ago. "As the Father has sent Me [to serve] so send I you!" Those stabbing, imperative words need to be taken very seriously today.

Our conduct pertains not only to our public deportment but also our private. For how we behave in our daily encounters is a sure indicator of what sort of souls and spirits we possess, and truly matters both before God and before men. But, it also matters to me. Do I honestly know without a shred of doubt that my little life is a noble tribute to God, my Father, in a world of woe?

We must come to see clearly, then, that our Father expects us to be benevolent people who diffuse pleasure wherever we are called to serve. In a sense we can be sincere souls who shine like real rainbows in the rough storms of life.

When at last our Father calls us home to be with Him, we should leave behind a legacy of love, goodwill and good cheer by which we are remembered. Few of us will ever lay much claim to fame in this world. But each of us can bring a touch of kindness and genuine concern to those we meet on the common crossroads of life.

This has always been Christ's intention for those who follow Him. He calls us into His family as His little children. He asks us to look with compassion on others. He encourages us in order that we in turn should also encourage each other on the tough trails we tramp with tears. He fills us with fresh hope that, by the same measure, we should inspire those around us with new hope amid their hardships. He fills us with His own glorious gladness, expecting that this delight and joy in Him will ignite others with His exuberance.

Spurgeon, that splendid British minister, once made the stirring comment, "He who climbs above the care of this world, and turns his face to his God, has found the sunny side of life."

And those who share the sunshine will be heartily welcomed by those who have grown weary and worn along the way.

Just recently, Ursula and I visited an elderly couple who live some distance away. I was not even sure I could remember how to get there so I dug out an old road map and traced on it the best route to follow across the foothills and through tangled streets. By dint of patient perseverance, we finally found their humble home.

A violent windstorm a few days before had created havoc in their neighborhood. I saw where a huge branch had crashed down on a red-tiled roof, tearing away the tiles and wrecking the structure. In front of our friend's home, another tree had been broken off by the blow. Piles of broken branches, litter, and debris were scattered across the yard. It was sad to see!

It was also a dreary day for the old folks who had fought so valiantly for so many years to establish their home in this tough spot. What they needed just now was a note of cheer and a few hearty chuckles to drive the fear away.

As we sat at their simple table, sharing a cup of tea with humble crackers and cheese, the old gentleman looked across at me, his face full of emotion. He was fighting back the tears, speaking in a choked voice, when he said sincerely, "Phillip, it is just wonderful, wonderful to have you back! You will never, ever know how much we missed you. You have always been such a dear, dear neighbor and friend to us. Thank you for coming again!" It was a poignant moment and had made the whole trip so worthwhile.

All of us had been renewed, refreshed, remade.

When we parted, it was with big, old-fashioned, warm bear hugs all around. A lovely farewell! In quiet joy we drove home in the warm glow of the setting sun. Our hearts say peace, peace, peace on earth! Goodwill toward men!

CHAPTER SIX

Health and Vigor

Health and vigor with which to relish life are among the most precious gifts from our Father. It is not until we are deprived of them that we realize their true value.

This simple, basic truth escapes most of us. We sort of assume that our general well-being just comes naturally. We often act and behave in a most casual manner in caring for our health. We abuse our bodies with impunity, not giving much heed to how they are nourished or sustained in the struggle to survive.

Yet as God's people we need both health and vigor, not only to be an honorable habitation for His Royal Presence, but also to be active agents on His behalf.

The other day a young, blond-haired woman, her hair flying in the wind, whipped past me in her car. On the back bumper in large letters was this astonishing slogan: EN-JOY BEING. In two five-letter words it summed up what this chapter is all about.

How can one *enjoy being* in a broken body?
How can one *enjoy being* when obviously obese?
How can one *enjoy being* as a pathetic patient?
How can one *enjoy being* if immobilized by drugs?
How can one *enjoy being* if unfit and unwell?

How can one *enjoy being* far below our best?

I know all the answers. I have heard all the excuses. I am familiar with all the lame jokes that deflect a serious self-appraisal. So people just go on neglecting their health, hoping doctors and drugs will help.

Health is a huge topic with endless implications that involve poverty, lack of nutritional information, ignorance about basic hygiene, governmental health schemes, the pollution of the planet, prevention of environmental pollution, food contamination, etc., etc., etc. In each of these areas there are already hundreds of books available. The hard, core question is, What can I do in the way of basic self-discipline to help maintain my own health and vigor?

For when all is said and done, in large measure, barring some awful accident or inescapable disease, my health and vigor pretty much depend on how I choose to live. No one else can make those choices for me.

As a youngster I grew up in one of the most disease-ridden regions of Africa, and there were few proper medical facilities available to the population. Malaria, rickets, tropical dysentery, typhoid fever, and a score of other scourges took a deadly toll of malnourished, underfed people.

I was constantly ill. Robust health was foreign to me. I came to think that being unwell was just part of being. Not until I moved to the cool, clean, and invigorating climate of Canada did I ever dream of what buoyant health could be.

After returning to Africa again, my fragile health quickly collapsed. At the youthful age of thirty-five I was examined by an elderly, wise, and godly physician. He looked at me with solemn and piercing eyes. "You are a young father with a family to care for. If you remain in the tropics you will be buried within six months. Get your affairs in order. Leave this country. Start to care properly for your own health!" That was forty years ago.

The ensuing years have not been easy years. My health has always been fragile. Like fine china, it fractures easily. To sustain my strength and energize my vitality, it has been imperative to seek guidance from Christ in how to live a healthy, wholesome life, one in which I could enjoy being, enjoy Him, enjoy serving my generation.

What follows are some guidelines for health and vigor that I have learned through many encounters with adverse circumstances. Perhaps the reader will not sneer if some seem too simple, but at seventy-five years of age, I feel very fit and, with energy from above, still carry a full workload.

Trust and Thank Our Father for Abundant Life

Christ assures us He came into the world that we might have life and live abundantly. If, then, we open ourselves to receive His vigor and stimulus, He will share His own dynamic energy with us. We must, of course, do our part. We must see to it that we are cleansed, and that we are willing to be purified by His incoming presence, day by day.

An acute inner awareness of His person, present with us and in us, deters us from endless defilement. We will then consider it an honor to have Him share life with us, to be His representatives here.

This intimate interaction with Him guarantees that my body is neither abused or misused. It is held in trust, honor, and dignified respect as His residence. I can, therefore, depend on Him to direct me in caring for my body in quiet compliance with His wishes. And in so doing, enjoy being His friend.

This implicit confidence in His constant care, not only as my Friend but also as my Great Physician, brings Him enormous pleasure. At the same time it empowers me as His follower with profound joy in His presence—an admirable stimulus to wholesome health and well-being in His company.

Live at Peace with God and Others

Buoyant health and vigor are produced by much more than mere physical fitness. There must also be an inner serenity of soul and quiet stillness of spirit. All must be well within.

Even though we live in a stress-ridden society, as God's people we must be at peace with Him. We choose not to fret and fume or fight about the circumstances of life in which He places us. With calm confidence in Him we just carry on quietly, thanking Him in every situation.

In our interaction with other human beings, we determine to look on them with care and compassion. We try with God's grace to accept others as they are. We forgive them for their folly, their faults, or their fickle ways just as our dear Father forgives us. Then peace prevails and calm repose refreshes our inner lives.

Eat Wholesome, Nourishing Food

This entire subject was dealt with in detail in my book *Taming Tension,* written twenty-five years ago. The principles stated there remain the same, and in large part they have contributed to my own health well into old age.

Most people in developed countries have ready access to fresh fruit, a wide variety of vegetables, whole grains, and other beneficial foods. What we shall eat and how we prepare it is of our own choosing. Sad to say, many people prefer junk food. Their diets are deficient in the basic nutrients needed to sustain bodily health and supply vigor for buoyant well-being.

This does not imply we become food faddists. But it does mean we eat plain, wholesome meals with plenty of fresh fruit, abundant fresh vegetables, nourishing whole grain breads and cereals, with proper portions of lean meat and fish. Nuts, milk, and cheese are beneficial in small servings.

For older people, vitamin and mineral supplements help prevent ailments that might arise from a less efficient digestive system. Learn to relish wholesome food.

Meals can be joyous occasions when one has a hearty appetite. And never forget to give thanks for the bounty of good food. There are millions starving, without good cause. Live simply in order that others may simply live.

Drink an Abundance of Pure Liquids

Our bodies are roughly seventy percent liquid. To maintain maximum body metabolism and general well-being, our intake of fluids must be maintained at a high level.

The very finest drink is plain, pure water. In many areas, water supplies are polluted: procure an efficient filter. But above all, drink plenty of water if you wish to be well. There is no substitute for this life-sustaining substance provided by our Father.

There are all sorts of alternatives offered, many that have a strong appeal to the palate. Soft drinks, sodas, wines, spirits, teas, and coffees are all marketed at enormous profit to a gullible, unsuspecting public. But most of these beverages are damaging to one's health and well-being. Only herb teas, taken in moderation, can be truly beneficial. As God's person, protect His residence.

If you truly desire a clear complexion, a clear mind, a clear digestive tract, a clear path to ample mobility, then drink an abundance of clear, clean water at a normal temperature. You will be astounded!

Decide Daily to Diligently Exercise Your Body

Despite all the deceptive blandishments of evolutionists, humanists, and secular scientists, the basic truth remains that our human bodies are of supernatural, divine design. Only the all-wise, eternal Father fully comprehends as we do not the amazing, complex, and intricate makeup of our beings. But we must all learn one profound principle: Be active! As the saying goes: Use it or lose it!

We in the West live in a sedentary society. Cars, computers,

TV screens may all be hailed as fine inventions but they have enslaved us to our seats and a soft lifestyle.

Be brave enough to break free from this bondage. Get up! Get outdoors! Get moving! Walk, hike, garden, swim, ski, skate, build a rock wall, and so build some solid muscle and tough tendons.

In this there is no substitute for self-discipline. No one else will do it for you, not even the living Christ. Just do it!

Get Outdoors for Fresh Air, Sunshine, and Fresh Views

For many years, I have urged readers to take the time to get outdoors, to get alone with our Father in the refreshing environment of His own creation. Let the sun lift your spirit in gratitude to Him. Inhale deeply of fresh breezes that recharge your whole being with oxygen-rich air. Allow your whole outlook on life to be gently renewed with wide views and new horizons.

All of us as His children need the healing balm of trees and grass, of meadows and mountains, of wind and waves, of singing streams and warbling birds, of sunset and sunrise. They are each beautiful bounties He bestows on us without fee and without charge. They can do you enormous good as you open your life, your soul, your spirit to the gentle touch of His Spirit.

Learn to know Him better in the still places. He loves to meet you in solitude.

Take Time to Rest, to Repose in Quietness

We live in a busy, boisterous, stressed-out society. A score of sounds assault our senses. As many other tensions put us under pressure, we must by a conscious action of our wills determine daily to withdraw from the chaos.

Find a quiet time to ponder long thoughts, to thank our Father for His care, to rest calmly in Christ, to find refreshment from the upwelling springs of His Spirit.

In quietness and in confidence you will be re-created by His presence, by His peace, by His power. Out of His very life imparted to you daily will come new health, great vigor, and His courage to carry on.

CHAPTER SEVEN

Taking Time to Think Quietly and Calmly

Because we live in a high-pressure world from which a hundred strident voices clamor for our attention, we must take time to be alone with God our Father to hear Him speak. It is imperative that we turn our attention to the truths delivered to us by Christ, both through His teaching and by His life. We must be still and sensitive in His own presence in order to be lead and instructed by His gracious, divine Spirit.

All of the foregoing is generally well known to most of us. We have been told these things often. The heart-searching question is whether or not we actually do it.

In this book about what really matters most in life, I wish to give my own personal witness to this wonderful constituent of life with Christ. Please understand I do *not* boast of a special inner piety. But I wish to declare to anyone who honestly hungers and thirsts to know the living Christ firsthand, it is possible within the privacy of our own souls.

I am aware that there are detractors who insist that this kind of awareness is some sort of mysticism or even fanaticism. But what I advocate is really the knowledge of Christ's presence in daily conduct. To help the reader understand just a little better, here are several other goals:

Getting alone with God
Being still before God's Spirit
Waiting on the Most High
Having the mind of Christ in mine
Being led by God calmly, hourly

Of course it takes time to do this in a practical, workable way. Most of us know full well that if we are to excel in any given area of life we must devote time, thought, and effort to it. If we are going to prevail in any profession, or art form, or athletics we must set aside other competing interests and devote our undivided attention to the one of supreme importance.

The principle is precisely the same in the realm of the soul and spirit. Christ calls us to follow Him, to be willing to come under His daily discipline and direction, to become subject to His divine orders: Following Christ is to heed His precise instructions. It is to carry out His clear commands. It is to obey His orders and to do His will in all goodwill.

Contemporary Christians are not at all eager about this sort of spiritual discipline. Rather they have more often been led to believe that loving God is like some sort of social activity in which they sing happy songs, clap their hands, sway to the rhythm, and shout for joy.

It is little wonder, then, that when things go wrong and their personal problems multiply, they are so easily discouraged. Instead of being strong, steadfast people with unshakable confidence in Christ, they cry the blues and look for someone else to blame for their troubles.

Our Father calls us to be a distinct and very different class of citizens. He expects us to live with calm confidence in Him. He longs to see us living an abundant life in His care as we quietly trust Him.

We can only do this in intimate communion with Him.

So it is essential for us to spend time, much time, alone in studying His Word. Let His gracious Spirit become your teacher, your mentor, your private tutor. He will lead you step-by-step into enduring truth. He will guide you into eternal, practical principles by which you can live in peace and power, amid a world of chaos.

I have discovered across a very long lifetime that the quiet hours in company with Christ are cherished times. It is then as I meditate over His statements and reflect on His commitments to me as His beloved, that His life, His interests, His outlook gradually become mine.

Spending time with Christ and meditating on His will is vital. There is no other way in which you can acquire the mind of Christ. There is no other way in which your emotions can come calmly under His control. There is no other way in which your wayward will can become submissive to His great, good will.

This is the supreme secret to walking with Him in harmony, holiness, and health of spirit and soul. It is the key to knowing Christ, trusting God your Father, and being led in joy and quietness by His Spirit.

I cannot overstate the simple truth that a man or woman whose life truly counts for Christ is a person who spends time alone with the living God in quiet communion and profound prayer. Giving Christ time and prayer is to honor Him, to give Him opportunity to impress His life on me.

I cannot give hours of each day to the TV screen, the computer console, or the daily newspaper, and then give God only ten minutes and expect to be His person who pleases Him. That is absurd!

I have endeavored under our Father's guidance to warn His people that unless we give Him first place in our lives, the world around us will command prior position in our thinking. It used to be somewhat of a secret that the mass media of the secular Western world was making a concerted effort to impose its own set of values on our society. Now it is common knowledge. That it has largely succeeded in the last half of this century can be seen in the chaos, confusion, and crime of our culture.

In large measure the problems of modern society are the result of God's people having never been taught by their leaders to take His commands seriously. To be a different and distinct people, we must have His mind-set and His outlook on life, to see life as Christ sees life with its transient values, wherein all that truly endures is of eternal worth.

The terrible, terrible tragedy of the twentieth-century church is its easygoing complacency. Too few of its prominent people have been deep thinkers with deep convictions. The fashionable, popular approach to most of the terrible problems of our decadent society is to go with the flow. Simply amuse the masses, entertain the crowds, be a producer of popular ideas and pop music that will pack the churches with worldly-wise worshipers. As long as the pulpit is popular and the crowds consider it to be "cool" to go to church, our leaders have assured themselves God is pleased.

But Christ calls us to a distinct sort of life. It is one of personal love and loyalty to Him. It calls for sacrifice and service to others. It demands integrity within.

The only possible way in which Christ can ever truly command our attention is to have a living encounter with us from day to day in the secret sanctum of our souls. He has never changed over the thousands of years that He has communed with man. Here are just a handful of His statements to us (emphasis mine).

> This book of the law shall not depart out of thy mouth; but thou shalt meditate therein day and night, that thou mayest observe *to do* according to

all that is written therein: for then thou shalt make thy way prosperous, and then thou shalt have good success [in pleasing God]. (Joshua 1:8)

Be *still* and know that I am God: I will be exalted among the heathen, I will be exalted in the earth. The LORD of hosts *is with us.* (Psalm 46:10–11)

But seek ye *first* the kingdom [rule] of God, and His righteousness; and all these things shall be added unto you. (Matthew 6:33)

Jesus answered and said unto him, "If a man love Me, *he will keep my words* [comply with my commands]: and my Father will love him, and we will come unto him, and make our abode with him." (John 14:23)

If ye keep My commandments, *ye shall abide in my love;* even as I have kept My Father's commandments, and abide in His love. (John 15:10)

Ye are My friends, *if ye do* whatsoever I command you. (John 15:14)

There is nothing vague or ambiguous about any of these plain, direct declarations from the living God. Our confusion comes from our own refusal to carry them out. We dredge up a dozen lame excuses for not complying with Christ's commands: they are neither practical nor workable in our modern world; we do not have the time to really think them through; the cost is too high; surely the God of all grace and goodness does not really call us to such severe and stern commitments. The list goes on and on!

Then we wonder why we are powerless people.

We wonder why we do not impact our generation.

We wonder why most of us are pagan people.

We wonder why our world is all awry.

Meanwhile Christ continues to call us apart, away from the chaos and clamor of our culture to spend time with Him in close communion. He asks us for our undivided attention. He invites us to be still, silent in calm solitude with Him so He can speak clearly to us. He expects us to respond to His requests in brave, bold, and forthright faith—not flinching or holding back. He bids us to count the high cost of being His friend. He tells us to think things through, to discover what endures and what is sheer vanity, human pride, and nonsense.

But most of us simply refuse.

To be godly takes time alone with God.

We are confident that casual church services are quite sufficient to be spiritual people.

But no! It is not church attendance that Christ calls us to—He desires close communion with us in the secret place; He wants our love.

I repeat here in earnestness what I have written about for more than thirty-five years. I tell you, the reader, in truth what I have told thousands of people in public. You must get to know God firsthand, in person, privately! He is real. He is alive. He is active. He is at work in the world. He invites you to meet Him alone. He comes seeking your acquaintance, your love, your loyalty.

The central question is, Do you wish to meet Him?

Have you seriously considered this matter?

Did you ever truly think it through?

Are you prepared to open your life to Him?

This is a serious, tough, life-changing act of your will.

Intimacy with Christ is much more than a bright idea. It is much more than a sentimental, emotional decision made in a moving moment of soft music or impassioned preaching.

It is a profound prayer of utter relinquishment to the Most High, in which you calmly, quietly, in genuine sincerity surrender yourself to Christ-God, very God, who stands before you with open arms and radiant smile as your personal Savior, Deliverer, and Emancipator.

He, and only He, God Himself, gives Himself to you as you in turn give yourself to Him. It is an exchange of life between Him and you. As you continuously partake of His life, you are in fact receiving the newness of His eternal life, which not only changes you, but also changes your entire personal relationship to Him.

You discover God is your heavenly Father.

You discover Christ is your dearest Friend.

You discover His Holy Spirit is your constant Fellow Companion and Counsellor in a complicated world.

You discover, at last, He is here. . . . All is well!

CHAPTER EIGHT

Hope for the Way

Those of us who have come to know the living Christ as our constant Friend and Companion have become people of bright hope. Our hope is not grounded on health or wealth or anything transitory. Rather, our hope is grounded in God our Father.

That statement is fairly easy to say.

Yet it is one of the most profound principles on the planet.

And few are the people whose entire conduct and calm assurance in life are dependent on the divine presence of the Most High and whose supreme hope is in Him.

One time a younger woman in great extremity, searching for a home, came to us amid her perplexity. As we stood in the compact kitchen of our humble apartment, I addressed her with unusual directness:

You simply cannot always rely on your friends.

You will find even the government can fail.

You may discover your family is not faithful.

You cannot always count on the church.

Everything and everyone is in flux and change.

In this world nothing endures forever.

Only the living Lord God never changes.

He is our only sure hope!

This may sound stern to someone in a time of trouble, but it is the bedrock upon which we can build our lives with absolute assurance. We may devote our days, and even our nights, to trying to cover all the bases in life. But nothing ever comes close to giving us the bright, shining hope that our Father gives us needed for the way.

Again, and again, and again I turn to Him and softly say, "Father, you are here. I'm in your care. All is well."

This calm confidence is not self-hypnosis. Nor is it some sort of delusion. It is in fact a quiet, deliberate act of my will, in which I choose to cultivate the companionship of Christ Himself at any and every point of pressure on the path of life.

It is utter folly to imagine that our little lives will somehow be free of trouble or tragedy. The Master told us emphatically on various occasions that in this earthly sojourn with Him each day would have its tests; the way would be fraught with tribulation; the trip could well be a tough trek.

But He did not leave us in despair.

He never does!

His assurance to us is such bright hope. "In this world ye shall have tribulation: but be of good cheer; I have overcome the world."

So we can be of good cheer on the condition we take life as He took it. He always looked on life here, no matter how harsh it was, as the way home to His Father! Always, always He was acutely aware of the supreme secret that the few years here were brief at best, even if they might be bruising, and that ultimately He was on His way to His Father.

This was His shining assurance.

This was His enduring inspiration.

This was His bright hope.

It is most moving to read carefully the last profound prayers and petitions uttered by Christ just before His terrible torment in Gethsemane, before He was in the presence of the cruel high priest, before He was at Calvary. As always, He comes to His Father for consolation and for confidence to carry on!

So with utmost earnestness I say to you, it matters most to see our few years here as the way to our Father. We are pilgrims, strangers, passing through a transient scene. Nothing lasts, nothing endures, but our gaze is fastened on our Father's face. His arms are always wide open to embrace us warmly. We actually are heading home. Nothing, no nothing, can shift us from a glorious, shining assurance in Him.

He Is Our Hope!

As a rather rough, tough, old mountain man, I have had more than my share of rocky roads and tough trails in a long life of struggling to survive. But I can fervently testify that ultimately it was my unshakable hope in God my Father that served as my lodestar. He made it possible to push on with courage and good cheer.

Not long ago a couple much younger than we are remarked to Ursula and I, "You two really are quite astonishing people. You have so much enthusiasm. You are so full of fun. You have the vigor of youth."

My only comment was a heartfelt, "Because our hope is in God Himself, He makes all the difference along the way!"

I am thoroughly familiar with all the cynical charges made against God's people: that they just believe in a pie in the sky; that trusting Christ is just a psychological crutch; that religion is just an opiate.

To all of which I have several simple responses.

Why then are nonbelievers so full of despair?

Why, when death is at the door, do you call for us?

Why are you constantly seeking but never satisfied?

Only the humble see their own inability to go it alone and turn to our Father for strength and hope for the way.

Daily I entreat Him for three special attributes, which only He can provide:

(1) "Father, kindly give me your courage to carry on just for today."

(2) "Father, in your compassion give me your patience to wait for your good time."

(3) "Father, in your generosity give me your grace to accept your arrangement of all my affairs!"

He Responds with His Presence, His Power, His Peace

He does not bestow the generous gifts of His person apart from or detached from Himself. Christ comes to us Himself, and in the person of His own gracious Spirit imparts to us His very own life, so that life burns bright with the lovely hope of His presence. That is the way in which I overcome all the troubles of this day and every other day.

Just moments after penning those lines, a compelling, irresistible, inner conviction came to me that I should drive over the mountains some thirty miles to see a younger couple I had not seen in two years. The gracious Spirit of Christ constrained me to set aside every other duty and go at once.

It was a glorious, midwinter morning with sharp sunlight illuminating every crag and ridge in bright light. In the frosty clearings, cattle were munching on dry hay scattered by ranchers. But vultures soared against the blue sky on dark wings. They were like an omen of the awful agony that would engulf this glorious day in grief.

The instant I drove into the barnyard, I was met by a stranger with the explosive news: "Their son of seventeen hung himself. His dad found him before sunrise this morning."

Softly I stepped into the sprawling old ranch house. It was full of neighbors, friends, and clergy who gathered in its grand old room and who had come to weep and console the family.

The moment the distraught parents saw me through their tears, they leaped to their feet, cried out in anguish, "Phillip—Phillip," then rushed over to fling themselves into my outstretched arms. They simply sobbed, unable to stop . . . utterly shattered . . . utterly crushed . . . utterly devastated.

"How did you hear? How did you know to come?"

They pressed me close. They hugged me. They clung to me. All I could reply was that God, my Father, by His gentle Spirit had sent me to them in His compassion, clean over the mountains, by His loving care.

In the darkness of that dreadful hour I was able to assure these two precious people that Christ Himself was here. He could set their spirits free. He could pour the healing oil of His Spirit into their wounded souls. He would, in His time, bring great good out of this awful anguish.

A comforting hope in God began to fill that huge ranch house. We wept together. We prayed together in the wondrous compassion of our Father!

Over and over the remark was repeated, "Today, in truth, we have seen a miracle of God's grace in sending you to us."

Softly I slipped out of the crowd and drove away, floods of tears streaming down my burning cheeks. But those tears were commingled sorrow and joy. For in the intense stillness of that sweeping mountain valley an acute, palpable awareness of Christ's presence was all around, on and over the earth.

He had come in person to touch each of us.

He had risen among us in incredible reality, with healing in His wings.

He had dispelled the darkness with the sharp, glowing light of His profound presence.

He had bound up the broken spirits. He had spoken peace to shattered souls. He had given hope.

He is the God of all hope! Our hope is in Him!

Out of that family's tragedy I am convinced Christ will bring renewed life, vigor, faith, and inspiration to that whole mountain region. The communities in which Christians gather in their little country churches will be energized, quickened, and encouraged to trust Him in new and wondrous ways. That is just His way of working in this shaky, old world.

Far too many of God's children in our churches have placed their hope in the same transient, unreliable, deceptive human devices as the world has. Government schemes, entitlement programs, health plans, security systems, investments, real estate holdings, banks, insurance companies, and even government bonds can betray us. They provide a false sense of security and empty hope against the ultimate end of men.

Why do I say this?

Who am I to fault all of man's finest plans?

Who do I trust for my ultimate, eternal care?

My trust, my surety, my hope is in God. He and only He makes full provision for my way both in this world and in the world to come.

Death is the great divide between the two worlds. Each of us, without exception, must pass through its narrow doorway in single file. In that hour of "passing on," all the impediments accumulated in our earthly journey must suddenly be jettisoned. None of it will do us a particle of benefit in the eons of eternity that lay ahead. Our possessions, our security measures, our wealth, our connections, our earthly resources are of no consequence.

When we recognize these realities, our whole value system changes. Suddenly the only question of consequence for eternity is, Do you know God as your loving Father and Christ Jesus, His Son, as your Friend, your Savior?

Only in this intimacy is there eternal life . . . His life.

Only in Him does anyone enjoy enduring hope.

Only He gives us hope here and hope there.

Only He provides such powerful assurance, for He is the way.

Across the many years that I have traveled the rocky road in life, it has been an honor, a joy, a delight to bring bright hope to fellow travelers by introducing them gently to the living Christ. Those who feared the future suddenly found enormous hope and calm confidence in Christ. He is our hope both here and in heaven ahead.

CHAPTER NINE

Relish the Beauty Around You

This book addresses that quintessential question of life, What makes life worth living? What experiences and what activities count most for time and for eternity? What truly pleases God, blesses others, and enriches our days?

One of the supreme answers is the title to this chapter. It is one of the sacred keys to a life of balance, serenity, and strength amid the tension and turmoil of our times. I have made frequent reference in this book to the increasing stress of living as God's people in the high pressure environment of our computer age.

Tension creates great gaps that are torn into the tapestry of our times. People are almost frantic in their pursuit of peace and quiet amid the rush and scramble to succeed. On the one hand, it often seems we are gaining ground in our search for serenity amid the mayhem of our feverish world. Yet for many, there is an emptiness that neither the TV screen, the daily newspaper, the telephone, nor any other technology can adequately fill—no, not even their work.

So let me offer a simple alternative. But it demands a sincere discipline of the soul. In short it calls for a sharp shift of attention. It takes a serious effort to focus on the remarkable beauty of the natural glories given to us daily by our Father. It means we must learn to give Him sincere gratitude for His generous inspiration. It comes to us without cost if we will but take the time to accept it daily from His good hand.

For it is He who creates and sustains the beauty of the earth.

It is man who often mars the world in which we live.

A case in point: It had been a hard and difficult week. There were endless complications in trying to get a local handyman to fix a few minor repairs in our home. Nothing serious, just waiting and waiting; hoping the fixer-upper would finally show up and somehow manage a few little jobs. Then there was a long-distance call from a publisher. The original manuscript I had sent to them had been destroyed by mistake. Then the drastic discovery that the only son of one of our dearest friends had ended his own life under the influence of drugs. The sorrow, anguish, and fragmentation of that family was horrendous.

Amid all this trauma and all this tension I needed more than pious platitudes or sweet sentiments. I desperately needed a personal touch from the living Christ to draw me away from all the heat and passion. So I went in search of solace in a long, quiet walk alone with my Friend, the living Lord, Christ.

It had rained gently during the night, but the dawn broke bright. From our wide windows we have sweeping vistas to the farthest horizons. Veils of crimson clouds floated in the sky above the rising sun. It was a moment to pause, to reflect, to rejoice, to give thanks for the uplift of the dawn.

As I stepped outside to start on my walk, the soft gentle notes of a mockingbird came to me across the green meadow beyond the road. In a parallel impression, the thought came surging into my soul, "Your Father cares for the birds, for the wild Johnny-jump-ups in the fields. He, too, cares for you. Be of good cheer!"

And in that instant I set out with vigor.

Suddenly, swiftly, smoothly all of my attention was centered in the loveliness of the natural world around me. The stresses of the week lifted from my spirit. The fresh, sweet, pungent fragrance of the hedges that hung heavy with raindrops tantalized my nostrils. I inhaled deeply of the oxygen-charged air. I took in draught after draught of the supercharged atmosphere around me.

The oxygen rushed through my lungs, cascaded into my bloodstream, into my body, my brain, my liver, my whole being. I was being quickened, energized, enlivened by abundant gifts of new life freely received from God my Father's generous hand. Spontaneously the phrases tumbled from my lips: "Thank You, Father! Thank You, Father! Thank You, Father!" These were sincere expressions of deep and genuine gratitude for all His goodness to His weary child, worn with a week of reverses.

My pace quickened! I was covering the ground in giant strides. My eyes grew bright and alight, sharp to see and enjoy and relish every tree, shrub, or flower that adorned this day. I spotted a worn mailbox on a wooden post. A luxuriant honeysuckle vine had grown up around and over the wobbly thing, wrapping it in a beautiful bouquet of delicate blooms. A gorgeous fragrance floated along the road. "That's just the way our Lord, the living Christ, loves to enfold our rough days in the tender embrace of His care."

I sensed such a buoyancy within that I could not help but smile. If it had not been so early in the day I would have started to sing for pure joy. But the folks still asleep might not have shared in my joy.

Oh the glory of my God! Oh the faithfulness of my Father!

Oh the companionship of Christ my Friend! Oh the sweet consolation of His gracious Spirit!

All just because I took the time to set out on a quiet walk with Him, relishing the beauty of the earth all around. Too, too often we have eyes that do not see, ears that do not hear, spirits that do not sense His presence with us on the crowded path of life.

As I walked softly through the quiet streets of this neighborhood, I could have been walking through any suburb of ten thousand towns on this continent. The only difference in this sacred hour was that I had set my soul to "see" the wonders of my Father's world all around me. I refused to allow my emotions, my mind, or my will to return to the tensions of the week.

In the splendor of the dawn, in the soothing call of a mockingbird, in the fragrance of fresh-fallen rain, in the sweetness of honeysuckle enfolding an old mailbox, an ordinary man had known again the tender touch of the Master's presence upon His child's aching spirit.

I came home from that walk refreshed, restored, renewed all because I had taken the time to relish the beauty and wonder of the world around me, the natural world adorned with beauty each day by our living Father to benefit His children.

All of this is free for the taking, for receiving as a gracious gift from the Most High.

Yet the tragedy is that so few ever avail themselves of this rich bounty from above. They turn instead to human help to find solace for their souls, convinced paying cash for counseling will mend their minds.

As someone who has lived over three-quarters of a century in our chaotic culture, I deem it my duty both to God, our Father, and to this generation to say that human counseling is no enduring cure for stressed-out souls. To believe that human philosophy, psychiatry, sociology, psychology, or any other man-made theory or therapy can bring solace and permanent healing to the human spirit is to indulge in self-deception.

All of these complex and confused human ideas for healing have spawned thousands of clinics and multitudes of therapists who endeavor to usurp the place and power of the risen, living Lord, Jesus Christ. Even in our churches, in our seminaries, in our seminars on recovery, in our so-called manuals on chemical addiction, everywhere and in almost every way men and women are encouraged to rely on human skills and human wisdom to do the divine work that only God Himself can do.

Our difficulty as a sophisticated, proud, self-centered people is that we prefer man's confusion to Christ's clear view. He calls us again and again and again back to the beautiful basics.

Look at the birds of the air on wing.
Look at the wild lilies in the meadow.
Look at the grass growing green.
Look at the lovely smile of a child.
Look at the sunrise and the sunset.
Look at the grain springing from the soil.
Look at the fruit tree bearing a crop.

Look—listen—learn!

But it is too simple, too humble, too childlike for us to comply.

Christ looked out upon his tension ridden generation and spoke these wondrous words. They have never, ever lost their power. They are as potent today as in His day.

Come unto me [the living Christ], all ye that labor and are heavy laden [with the stress and strain of life], and I will give you rest [repose, renewal]. Take

my yoke [my way of bearing life's burdens] upon
you, and learn of me; for I am meek and lowly in
heart [living in quiet humility]: and ye shall find rest
unto your souls. (Matthew 11:28–29)

But, sad to say, most of us simply do not believe Him. It
sounds so sweet and serene yet we spurn it.

In our arrogance and pride we reject His gentle invitation
to come to Him and find our remedy. Instead, the majority
feverishly choose to pursue the vain and foolish professors
of human wisdom. Do we wonder why our institutions are
so skewed? Do we marvel at the madness of our media?
Are we surprised at the decadence of our civilization? Are
we frightened by the fragmentation of our society?

Amid all the anguish of our times, a tiny handful of God's
children still respond to Christ's call: "Come and find calm
repose in my company." They know what it is to be still in
the solitude of His sublime creation, and know that he is
God, the eternal one. They know what it is to look lovingly
at the hills and mountains and sense in spirit that their help
comes from God their Father. They know what it is to watch
the birds build their nests and raise their broods, aware that
He who cares for sparrows also cares for them.

It is in this calm confidence in Christ that they are serene, sure, and strong.

There is about the natural world an element of
endurance and continuity not found in the tempestuous
ever-changing confusion of human civilizations. We human
beings in our misguided, self-assured wisdom often rape
and ruin the earth in greed and excess exploitation. The
whole cry of the environmental movement expresses
concern and outrage at the steady destruction of the biota,
the plight of endangered species, the awful devastation of
forests, grasslands, streams, lakes, seas, and lovely
landscapes. And so should we! Much of my youth and

strength was spent in the struggle to save our natural resources. They must not be depleted simply because they are expendable!

Though our natural resources might appear to endure, they do diminish. Yet even in their extremity they stand as reminders of our Father who designed them in magnificent order. They humble us with their exquisite beauty brought into existence by His magnificent mind. They turn us toward Him in deep gratitude for all the sublime inspiration they bring to our spirits. They still our souls in wonder, awe, and peace as we sense and see and experience His presence in every place.

The golden Johnny-jump-ups emerge into new life every spring from dry and barren ground. The sun tints the eastern and western skies with amazing beauty day after day. Wild blossoms fill the air with rare perfumes year after year. Glorious clouds grace the heavens. Mountains and hills are mantled in snow. From their slopes surge the streams and rivers and lakes. Birds and beasts adorn the weary old world in flight and form.

Get out, take time, relish the beauty about you. All of it is a stimulus to the seeking spirit, the searching soul. Our Father communes with His child in the natural world, which is His sanctuary. Meet Him there!

CHAPTER TEN

Giving Thanks Always

No other human activity can inject so much joy into life as simply giving thanks. By this I am not referring to just habitually saying grace at meals for good, nourishing food. Rather, the giving of thanks in all things, in all times, is a perpetual attitude of gratitude.

The reader may wonder why anyone would even take the time, much less a whole chapter in this book, for such a simple subject. The truth is, it is not always easy to give thanks. And blessed as we are, to our shame many of us do not give thanks, either to God our Father or to others, for our good fortune.

In part this is because a great many people feel sure they have *it* (whatever *it* is) coming to them. They are convinced that their contemporary society, with its overly beneficent governments, is responsible to provide for them. And, whatever the need, someone somewhere will supply it.

This feeling of entitlement explains the cynicism so common everywhere.

It accounts for the blatant lack of gratitude.

It is why people blame everyone but themselves for trouble. No wonder so few assume personal responsibility for their own well-being.

Ultimately it has produced crowds of malcontents.

Yet in this sort of world, with this sort of mind-set, Christ calls us to be content in His care, to give thanks for all things, and to share our genuine gratitude both with God our Father and others.

Most of us have no idea what profound pleasure our thanks bring to the Most High. Nor do we know what an enduring benefit it is to others to show them our thanks.

To give thanks is at heart an act of humility. It shows that people are not so self-absorbed that they fail to appreciate the favors, help, and benefits bestowed upon them by others. It means nothing is simply taken for granted. It indicates clearly that we are aware of the generosity, care, and kindness that flows to us from our Father and from other fellow human beings.

Giving thanks really is a beautiful behavior.

Not only does it nourish the well-being of others, but it blesses God Himself.

By giving thanks all of life is made to glow.

So by it we, too, learn to grow in goodwill.

It can become a daily delight, in which I literally determine to look for the silver edge.

And I learn to live on that edge.

Life lived with gratitude becomes a benediction. It is no longer a bore. It is not a burden. It is a chance to find the gems of God's grace sparkling like sequins among the otherwise tattered tapestry of life. We never know what a day will produce in our little lives, but we can be sure that if we search with sensitive spirits we can find fragments of precious moments and generous actions that deserve our genuine gratitude.

It is not enough to just recognize these benefits, which tumble at random into our experiences. We must take the time to contemplate them, to relish them, to actually see that people care enough to trouble themselves on our behalf, even in the most simple ways. Having done that, they deserve our verbal, tangible thanks.

This may mean taking the trouble to see them personally to give our true thanks. It may require a hearty, happy phone call filled with appreciation. It may involve taking the time to pen a few paragraphs of honest gratitude and true thanks for the favors bestowed.

Too often, far too often, these humble gestures are dismissed with a shrug of the shoulders and the casual comment, "Oh, why bother; they know I'm thankful." But the terrible truth is most people do not know—unless you tell them so!

Intimate, interpersonal giving and receiving of thanks is one thing that matters most in our tough, old, hard-boiled world. It is like a superb lubricant that reduces the wear and tear of our short sojourn here. It is the smooth oil of gracious goodwill that diminishes the rub of living and puts a shine on the daily routine.

I am always astonished at how even total strangers light up, smile, come alive, and expand with good cheer when I take the time to show them gratitude. It may be the teller in a bank; the checkout person in a busy supermarket; the attendant who pumps gas and cleans the windshield of my car; the gardener who trims the trees, mows the lawns, or plants some petunias along the sidewalk.

Each of us needs to feel appreciated.

Each of us needs some recognition.

Each of us blooms better when refreshed with thanks.

Simply put, I am saying be generous. Be gracious with your gratitude. Scatter praise, thanks, and approval across the day and all across your way.

This sincere action will lift other lives, stir other spirits, inspire other souls and fill your own with a song. It is a great, great good that any of us can do. Then all our little worlds will be brighter and better for it.

In giving thanks continually, under all circumstances, for all things, with all sorts of people who cross our path, we are performing our Father's work in this world. This profound principle of spiritual life eludes most people completely. But if you can grasp it in these pages, your entire life can take on a brand new dimension of divine delight.

Christ Himself, when He lived among us as the man Christ Jesus, stated clearly that when He worked He constantly gave thanks to His Father for also working in Him, with Him, through Him. He told His associates, and He tells us, that His work is not just His alone: it is His Father's work. He and His Father are one in going about doing great good—blessing multitudes, healing, cheering, helping, inspiring, touching the tormented, bringing hope, joy, and good cheer.

Then, having lived in that lovely way, He turned to His devoted disciples and declared that "as the Father has sent me into the world of men, now so do I send you out into that same weary world." In short, if men and women are to see and understand anything of our Father's character and conduct they will have to get a glimpse of God in us.

No wonder it is such a noble honor to be called a son of God! Little marvel that Christ's call to be His devoted follower is such a high calling. He appoints us to be His ambassadors of goodwill to our generation. Royal work indeed!

It is He who enables us to live out His purposes here and now.

Christ calls. Christ chooses. Christ commissions. I come under His command. I submit to His control. I carry out His clear instructions. This is what it means to do His will!

Churches and church leaders seem to emphasize the idea that somehow, in some super-spiritual way, we have to discover God's will for our lives. It is as if there was some obscure, hidden, secret design God has ordained for your career or your personal, private performance. The result is we miss the mark of a truly humble child of God in just doing the simple, lowly task of touching another life with His compassion today.

In my long lifetime of earnestly following the Master, I have discovered that He does not ask me to be sensational.

He does not ask me to be spectacular.

He does not ask me to be super-spiritual.

These may be the world's measure of success, but not His!

Instead, He asks me to do the simple, humble, ordinary things anyone can do who shares His life: the little gestures of gratitude and thanks, a sincere smile, and a helping hand.

Over and over He spoke of showing love and care and good cheer to our neighbors. He mentioned compassion for children, animals, and the poor. He spoke of cups of cold water. He told us not to forget the forlorn, those imprisoned in the dungeons of their loneliness, fears, or poverty. He told us to share freely of our bounties, for we have in fact received all we possess from His own generosity. So to pass it on really is an honor and joy.

Freely you have received: Now freely give!

Recognizing God's gracious giving is the supreme secret to giving thanks. When it dawns on our dull spirits that in actual fact all we have and all we are come from our Father's generous provision, we will be overwhelmed with genuine gratitude, glad to share our blessings with others.

In our sharing and in our daily deportment, let it be known that the very life of the living Christ is flowing through us to refresh and quicken the world we touch. Just as every beautiful benefit and glorious gesture of goodwill that comes to me is a clear demonstration of my Father's care, now in turn others sense and see that He is enriching their lives through my simple, sincere conduct.

Only He can make my emotions uplift the downcast.

Only He can use my mind to enlighten other minds in doubt.

Only He can so set my will to serve others in sincerity.

For you see, it is God Himself, in Christ, by His own Spirit who works in me both to will and to do His good pleasure day after day—if I let Him!

All of life then becomes a magnificent adventure with my Father. I trust Him quietly to direct all my decisions. I speak to Him intimately, openly about everyone I encounter. I constantly give humble, hearty thanks for putting such a sharp edge on all the everyday events. This is to know firsthand the delight of His abundant life.

Recently I drove through a torrential storm of rain and wind to visit a couple in great grief. Their yard was sodden with the storm. The whole house seemed so dreary. I knocked on the great, dark door. There was no immediate response. I waited and waited. Then I heard faint footsteps. A woman, the housekeeper, opened the door a crack to tell me the owners were away.

I asked if I could come in and just write a brief note to leave with her saying I had been there. As I did this the housekeeper suddenly began to pour out a terrible tale of woe and trouble in her own life. In an instant I knew our Father had sent me there just for her!

Quietly I asked her to sit down at the bare wooden table where I had begun to write. In a profound, personal encounter she was gently introduced to Christ who was present there to meet her in person.

And she was profoundly moved by the experience. Over and over again she would interrupt our conversation with some such remark as, "All my life these verses had been in my head. Now suddenly they have come alive in me."

A look of astonishment, ecstasy, joy would sweep across her features. "Now, for the first time the Word of God is really quickening me. I understand what He is saying to me. After all these years I can truly trust Him!"

Outside, the rain came down in solid sheets, blocking

out the sun, the light, the radiance of day. But in that darkened room the brilliant beauty of our Father's care and loving concern for this despondent woman swept away the darkness. The glory of His grace, the effulgence of Christ's forgiveness and friendship, the sweet solace of His Spirit filled this sad and forlorn soul to overflowing. She erupted in gratitude and thankfulness.

"Thank you so much! Thank you for coming here today!" It was our Father who in that sacred hour had touched this torn spirit and, having heard her cry, gave her His rest—a rest of soul she had never ever known before.

As I drove home, with the rain pounding on the roof of my truck, I too could only whisper in sublime joy, "Thank you, Father, for filling my own life with pleasures evermore. You are here. You are near. You are so dear!"

This sort of simple service and gratitude makes life so very rich!

CHAPTER ELEVEN

Goodwill, Good Cheer, Contentment

Much has already been said in this book about expressing goodwill and good cheer to others. It makes an enormous difference in our interaction with others and in our own inner contentment. Unfortunately, for many of us who consider ourselves to be God's children, contentment is not always a hallmark of our conduct.

In living, moving, working, and associating with multitudes of people drawn from many denominations it has surprised me to find that so many are restless, dissatisfied, and quite discontent. Very often they are quick to find fault, prone to harsh criticism, and apt to complain loudly about their lot in life.

There are real, solid causes for this regrettable attitude. If we understand them we can overcome them and find new ways in which to be content with what our Father chooses to bestow on us from day to day. For it matters much whether or not we are sweet-spirited people of goodwill and good cheer.

One cause of our discontentment is the constant

bombardment from the high-pressure civilization we live in. The entire industrial and commercial community is intent on increasing consumer demand for its products. The strategy of most advertising is to convince us that what we already have is not adequate or sufficient.

It is a subtle form of constant coercion that comes into our homes and minds through the media. If you give undue time and attention to the TV screen, to radio broadcasts, to newspapers, to the flood of flyers, to the glossy magazines you subscribe to, you will be bombarded by an enormous emphasis on making you want something more.

In the past, advertising focused on material things—a better home, a more luxurious car, a new wardrobe, a more handsome set of furniture, more exotic meals. You had to be convinced that you deserved these things. And the way to acquire them was, of course, to use the easy credit extended to you. Many times there was even no need for money down; you simply took delivery with the commitment to pay later. You had unwittingly stepped into the cruel trap in which you would twist and turn for years trying to discharge your debts.

This is not the way to live a content life!

More recently, with more leisure, shorter work weeks, and an increasingly mobile population living the "good life," the emphasis has shifted to leisure and pleasure. Travel, adventure, luxurious resorts, flights of fancy to faraway places, all sorts of sporting events and athletic activities entice people to do—go—be, never content with what is close to home, more convenient, and within their budget.

All of which may seem the "in thing to do." But more often it leaves people unhappily out of sorts and out of cash.

Now at the close of this century, standing on the tantalizing threshold of the twenty-first century, the new rage of the new age is for more and more information. The cyber-wise men with their gigantic information highways promise people access to endless knowledge, power, and pleasure on the Internet. It is all there for the taking, provided you acquire the latest equipment to exploit the resources.

Millions upon millions of gullible consumers are now totally convinced that getting on-line is the ultimate path to self-fulfillment. Little wonder we live in a world of chaos and confusion, bereft of contentment.

The incredible tragedy is that, for the most part, the world system has succeeded in seducing so many of God's people. Those in the church are really not much different from their contemporaries in the secular world. We have very much the same priorities, the same interests, the same success syndrome, the same old emphasis on treasures, leisure, and pleasure. We have been coerced into a lockstep of confusion and discontent, yet scarcely know it.

Christ Himself spoke very emphatically to this whole social phenomenon. In very blunt terms, He told the man disputing his inheritance with his brother, "Beware of covetousness: for a man's life consisteth not in the abundance of the things which he posesseth" (Luke 12:15), be they material assets, pleasurable pursuits, or the power that ostensibly comes from knowledge and information.

All of which puts us in the position of making hard choices and difficult decisions. Are we prepared to part ways with a world system that deludes us into believing it has the secret to success and fulfillment? Are we willing to walk quietly, calmly with our Father in contentment, even though others charge us with being disconnected? Are we brave enough to buck the trends of our times?

These are tough questions, and asking them may make me very unpopular. For many will sneer and scoff at my call to a simple, humble, quiet life of contentment in company with Christ. They insist that to live this way is "to lose touch." Yet the fact that will not go away is: One cannot be a friend to the world and its ways and at the same time be a friend to our Father and walk in His way. They are separate paths!

He, the Eternal One, in His Word declares very clearly: "A little that a righteous man has is better than the riches of many wicked" (Ps. 37:16); and "Godliness with contentment is great gain" (1 Tim. 6:6). The sad truth is, most of us are not satisfied to live this way.

It matters much that we should be. Otherwise we cannot be people of goodwill or good cheer.

It is essential to be content with what we have, with whatever our Father has bestowed upon us at any given point in time or place.

Yet for many of God's people, contentment is difficult to achieve. So often they feel deprived, while others around them seem to thrive. They think they are poor while others appear to prosper. They even consider themselves forsaken when others are fulfilled.

Perhaps I can be helpful here. Remember, contentment demands a divine, godly perspective, one of proper proportion. So take the long view of life. It is a journey. It is a pilgrim's path. We really are on the road home to be with our Father forever.

Along the way there are bound to be some bountiful, beautiful interludes. Our Father delights in supplying us with lovely bonuses. But by the same measure we can fully expect to encounter some tough terrain and trying times. It is inevitable that there will be difficult days of deep distress. We never know what a day will bring. Life is like that. It may be no better than living in a fruit picker's shack without any plumbing or it could be living in a pleasant home, high on a hill. My wife and I have lived in both.

The questions that matter most are, "Am I content with where I am? Do I find delight in my Father's place for me? Do I rest in His arrangement of my short trip through life?"

If indeed, in honesty and in sincerity, I can say yes to these searching questions, I hold the key to contentment within my grasp. For in saying yes I share in God's outlook on life. It is to see the whole chaotic world through which I travel with clear eyes and sincere spirit. For my Father is here with me always!

Out of this intense, acute, intimate awareness that the living Christ accompanies me at all times, there springs up within my soul His refreshing life of joyous good cheer. He is the eternal source of my strength, my serenity, my joy. It is the calm, sure, unshakable realization that God my Father gives me His own gracious Holy Spirit to abide with me that produces this goodwill within. He is present to impart His power, His peace, His profound direction in all I do. He guides in the details of each day, so I am willing and able to do His own good will.

The presence of the eternal, enduring, energetic God Almighty is the very ground of my being. In other words, in Him I live, and move, and have my true being. No longer am I just a bit of flotsam flung up on the foam, froth, and folly of a feeble man-made world. Instead I am a soul, unshakable and unafraid, rooted and grounded in God my Father.

This gives enormous surety and stability to my spirit. It is possible and practical for my little life to produce eternal, enduring fruit of great goodwill, no matter where He places me. Any spot, then, can become blessed, holy ground, where I can blossom and produce a harvest that honors Him.

What follows is a demonstration of whether or not a person can find goodwill, good cheer, and calm contentment in the midst of adversity. In this account of a particularly hectic time, perhaps the reader will see that I do not just write about tantalizing theory or high-sounding theology.

Ursula and I had made detailed plans for her to take a long trip up north in midwinter to address some rather important business decisions. She would be away several weeks. During her absence we had made special arrangements to have some alterations made to our little apartment. On top of which, it was my intention to place an important book manuscript in the hands of a publisher. So it was to be a busy time for both of us.

Without burdening the reader with boring details, let it just be said that nothing worked out as hoped. First, we lost all telephone connection because of an electrical failure. Second, the tradesman who was to do the work in our apartment simply never showed up—an absolute mystery. Third, the original manuscript sent to the publishers was somehow destroyed by mistake: the first time this has ever happened to me in over fifty years of writing.

Then, as if all of this was not enough, suddenly one night I became very ill, all alone at home. I could not even reach the bedroom. Lying stretched out, comatose, on the front room couch, it seemed my call home had come. So in quietness I gave my life calmly to Christ's care.

At long last the next day did dawn. But my strength was spent. I could scarcely cross the room without holding onto a chair, table, or door. It seemed I was done, and all of life was suddenly very much at a dead standstill.

Or was it?

Things are not always as they appear!

Especially when He, our Father God, is here.

Lying flat on my back, hardly able to move, with no appetite to eat or make any plans, I quietly asked Him to use this interlude in life to still touch others. I was also bold enough to believe He could again restore my strength and energy to honor His own mighty name!

To my joy, during this difficult week there was a remarkable sense of His presence with me. A powerful peace sustained my soul. Though all our plans were at a standstill, He was very much at work in the situation.

To my astonishment and delight, within just a few days it was again possible to enter deeply into the lives of others. I was able to share in their distress and to bring them goodwill. He was bringing great good out of my trouble. And, in that awareness, came quiet contentment.

Added to that, day by day, in fact hour by hour, He has restored my strength. Without ambulances, emergency wards, doctors, nurses, hospitals, or prescriptions, He has made me whole again. His name be honored.

Because He is here, let me say it again and again, all is well. Thank you, Father!

CHAPTER TWELVE

Freedom—Set Free to Follow Christ

One of the great catchwords of the world is freedom. The idea of personal liberty mesmerizes the multitudes. Somehow we are sure democracy sets us utterly free.

In truth, freedom is a double-edged concept. On the one hand, our constitutions do guarantee us the right to pursue our own personal happiness, as well as the liberty to do as we choose. These magnificent manifestos for modern man have drawn millions of men and women from countries where common people suffer under the tyranny of dictators or the oppression of corrupt civilizations. The quest for freedom has stirred the spirits of those who feel shackled in poverty or privation of any kind.

But the other side of our cherished freedom is that we are deceived into believing that our personal liberty is sacrosanct. As individuals, we are convinced that we have the right to decide exactly what we shall do with our lives. So much so, we insist that we, and only we, make all the decisions that determine our destiny. Simply stated: "I am convinced that I, and only I, have the right to myself." This means that men and women are free to choose what they will do, where they will go, what they will be, what they will say!

We in the Western world of the great democracies have applauded this idea of personal freedom for centuries. It is hailed as a titanic liberating force in our world. It has a way of dazzling us with pure pleasure, for it sets us afire to pursue our own aims and ambitions with fierce determination.

I was one of those who came to North America as a youth full of dreams, who would get caught in this web of woe.

Just as an unsuspecting bee or butterfly drawn to the shining, silver, spider's web shimmering in the morning sun suddenly finds itself in the entangling strands, so was I snared by the glittering strands of my society. The terrible tragedy was I did not realize the desperate danger in which I struggled to survive.

Well-meaning mentors, some of them ostensibly godly people, had unknowingly contributed to my captivity by our so-called free culture. Here are just a few of their fascinating fabrications that inflamed my mind and set my soul on a path of self-imprisonment.

"You owe it to yourself to succeed in business!"

"Go for the top. Let nothing stop you!"

"Plan your work. Then work your plan!"

"You're free to be whatever you wish!"

The list goes on and on.

It was heady stuff for an already headstrong youth.

I was convinced it was the road to independence.

I was king in my own domain, boss in my own affairs.

Month by month, year by year, endeavor by endeavor, I worked, worried, and wrapped myself ever tighter into that wretched web of deception that I was a free man. In actual fact, I was completely caught up in the dreadful despair of self-serving, self-satisfaction, self-centeredness. I had been deceived by the world!

I had become snared by the world's value system under the glittering guise of freedom and success. It had all been so attractive, so ambitious, so appealing. Yet in the end, none of it satisfied the deep yearnings of my soul. It was a spirit snared in selfishness wanting to be set free.

I had become a slave to my own drives and desires.

I twisted in torment in the strands of success.

I longed to be free from the folly and vanity of my own pride.

The stirring saga of how my captivity eventually was broken by the boundless grace of God my Father, has been told in the book *Wonder O' the Wind.* Oh the compassion of Christ Himself to come to me in living reality to set me free. Never, ever, shall the memory dim of that unforgettable day when His gentle Spirit so convicted me of my total imprisonment, that in utter capitulation I gave all of myself—all of my soul, all of my spirit, all that I was or had—completely into Christ's care and control.

For me that was a monumental moment.

It was the hour of deliverance.

I had passed over the great divide in life.

I was gloriously free to follow Christ anywhere.

I was calmly conscious of my Father's care.

His Spirit would now guide in a new way.

The idea of yieldedness needs to be explained here a little. For this so-called spiritual surrender of the soul absolutely eludes most people. Many in the church assume it is possible to be set free to serve both our own interests and God's interests. They boast openly about their liberty in the Spirit as if they are free to do as they choose. This is a dreadful delusion. It simply is not so!

Christ made it very clear that we can serve only one master in undivided loyalty and love. And only He, by the transforming power of His person and His presence within us, can ever deliver us from our dreadful self-delusion of being free—when in fact we are fettered to our own folly, our own pride, our own vanity, our own emptiness.

It is only the divine dynamic of Christ's own life and light and love that can lift the scales from our darkened spirits so we can see we are slaves to sin, to Satan, to ourselves! And the instant that happens we cry out like Saul on the Damascus road, "Oh Lord, what wilt Thou have me do?"

The gentle, calm reply is always the same: "Follow Me." Follow Christ away from the folly of man's wisdom. Follow Christ away from the vanity of the world. Follow Christ away from the snares of success. Simply, quietly, calmly trust Him to lead in the paths of righteousness and contentment under His care.

Following Christ is what makes life worth living!

It leads to an abundant, adventuresome life of close
Companionship with the living Christ.
It is a challenging call to serve Him and others
In courage and gracious goodwill.
As His follower I am His disciple, prepared to live
In devotion and divine discipline
Under His royal command.
Christ calls me to have complete confidence in
His control of my life . . . To trust in His
Goodwill as I live to do His bidding.
This is to live with joy and enthusiasm in Him.

The above describes a lofty life. It is a noble way to live. It is not just good fun and food and hearty fellowship, which so many church leaders promote. Nor is it a "happy hour" sort of spirituality in which I sing little songs over and over in a semi-hypnotic state, clapping my hands, swaying to the rhythm, feeling sure this delights the Most High. This sort of sensual emotionalism may very well stimulate or even sedate the masses. But it is not that deep inner life of serious devotion to God my Father that He looks for among His children.

He invites me to come apart from the crowds.

He bids me to choose freely to follow Him.

He assures me I am His, He is mine—Enough!

I am fully aware that the idea of finding complete freedom by submitting fully to Christ is difficult for many to grasp. In large part because their spiritual leaders and mentors have never entered into close communion with Christ. No pastor, no preacher, no teacher, no evangelist can ever lead God's people to find their utter freedom and total fulfillment in our Father's care, unless they themselves have experienced this emancipation.

Jesus Himself stated categorically that "If the Son shall set you free, you shall be free indeed!" It is one of the most quoted statements Christ ever made. It is also one of the least understood. Simply because so many of our mentors are still chained to our culture, still enslaved by the vain value system of our society, still deceived and deluded by the razzle-dazzle of our world and its ways that lead to destruction.

So if we are to honestly encourage people to embrace this new-found freedom that Christ offers, we must discover firsthand what it does to enhance and uplift our little lives.

Our Father never defrauds us. When He asks us to commit ourselves to His care and to His control, be assured He in turn commits Himself to our care and to our well-being.

This is what it means to live within His goodwill. Too many of us feel that to do God's will is bondage. We will very soon find out there is enormous joy, goodwill, and well-being in just doing His bidding. Why? Because everything He ever devises for our lives is intended for our good.

So when I freely, gladly, heartily decide to set my will to do His good will I enter an amazing, real experience of deep delight in Him. My life is no longer a drag—no longer drudgery—but a life of delight.

What I have just said is not high-sounding rhetoric intended to impress the reader. It reflects the day-to-day adventure of my own walk with God, and it produces enormous freedom from fear and frustration and futility.

First of all, there is pure pleasure in sensing and seeing Him do gentle, gracious things in the ordinary events of my life. I am a simple, common man of rough and ready makeup. Still I marvel at the edge of excitement Christ generates within my ordinary experiences. He literally fills them to overflowing with a touch of awe and wonder! The zest of youth has not diminished.

Someone who had not seen me for quite a long time remarked the other day, "You are still so young at heart, so full of enthusiasm, so free in spirit." If this is indeed so, it is in large part because I simply revel in His care, free from worry and concern because my Father is faithful to me as His son.

There is a second remarkable dimension to this life of liberty in Christ. He sets me completely free from the fret and fever of wondering what to do next. He provides clear direction in every step I must take. In His company He leads, I follow. He gives the specific directions. My part is to comply in calm confidence and quietly carry them out. It is all simple and straightforward. No confusion. No chaos!

Many of my friends and associates are often a bit baffled by this lighthearted lifestyle in His company. So I try to explain that I am a man under command. My life is really not my own to decide! That is done for me by my Father's divine and dependable direction. So in fact, in quiet faith in Him, it is possible to live a carefree life. This is real freedom!

Thirdly, there is a profound, precious, personal dignity that emerges in the companionship of Christ. It is not a

point of pride. It is not an abrasive arrogance of pretending to be pious. It is not a matter of boasting about being
super-spiritual. Rather, it is a secret sense of sublime self-
worth because I am His.

As I have said scores and scores of times to deeply
troubled souls, "It is not who you are that matters. It is
whose you are that truly counts for all time!" I am His! He
is mine! That freewill giving of each to the other is the love
that binds us together in unbreakable devotion. That element lends enormous dignity and self-worth to me as His
man. It is not that I am, nor do I pretend to be, a great guy.
But I know, I love, and I honor my great and loving God.

Fourthly, the divine dimension of freedom in Christ
means so much to me. By that I mean that to live in Christ's
company is to see clearly that He is present in all the affairs of my ordinary life. He brings purpose and significance
into the events of each day, for He shares them with me.

Always, always, there is this acute awareness: Christ is
here! He can bless! He can guide! He can turn water into
wine! He can calm the storm and bid the wild winds to be
still! He is here, I need not fear! He is my Friend!

No other simple assurance in all of this weary, dispirited,
cynical world can inject such freedom into my soul. My
spirit soars in the pure joy of His presence. In Him I find
power, peace, and pleasure of true freedom from all fear.
That is what matters most!

CHAPTER THIRTEEN

Friends Found in Great Books

As most of my readers know, I grew up in the rather remote, frontier environment of East Africa. As a small child there were no suitable schools for me to attend for hundreds of miles. In their loving concern for my well-being, my parents introduced me at a very early age to good books.

Because I had no surviving siblings and my only playmates were rather wild African youngsters, both Dad and Mother decided reading should become an active and powerful influence in my young life. Dad went to great trouble and expense to purchase fine books on such subjects as exploration, travel, wildlife, and outstanding Christian men. Mother taught me to read well at a very early age.

Both of them, it seemed, were far too busy with the great needs of their burgeoning mission work to spend much time with me. So I turned to books to find new friends and the companionship of rather remarkable people portrayed on their pages. Many, many treasured times were spent in

99

my tiny bedroom under the gables of our frontier home, lost in the high adventure of great men who had written great books and lived truly noble lives.

People like David Livingstone, Carl Akeley, Teddy Roosevelt, Cherry Kearton, Martin and Osa Johnston, as well as many others, were as well known to me as my own parents. As I spent uncounted hours reading and rereading the adventures of my boyhood heroes, they became in truth my dear and respected friends.

Nor has the passion for reading ever diminished across the long span of my own adventuresome life. Always, always, fine books by noble people have been my friends.

It would be no great hardship for me to be deprived of the telephone, the television, or almost any other modern technological device. But to be deprived of fine books would be a catastrophe. It is within their wisdom and joyous wonder that my mind, my emotions, and my entire spiritual life is often quickened, inspired, and set aflame with fresh enthusiasm.

Not only my human father, but also my heavenly Father bestowed on my entire life an enormous, ongoing benefit through great books. I have drunk deeply and fully from their fountain of inspiration. Good books reassure me that all is not lost in our sin-driven society with its violent crimes and cruel conduct.

Here and there Christ still calls out stalwart souls with brave spirits who will not be swayed or swept away in the corruption of our culture. They dare to be totally different from the world around them. They are bold enough to put their thoughts, their ideals, their visions, their noble ideas, which come from God Himself, upon the printed page for anyone to read and consider.

It takes courage to write a book of high virtue. It will not always win praise or approval from a skeptical, cynical society. But it certainly claims attention, and in many instances Christ uses these books to impact an entire generation with a clear view of what matters most.

There is an intimacy and personal privacy associated with reading a truly noble book. The hours spent in perusing its pages can be very precious. Passages that stir the spirit and strengthen the soul can be read and reread. The print can be underlined, marks made in the margins, personal notes scribbled on the page. Oh yes, books become special friends turned to often for cheer.

I well remember the day I was given a leather-bound copy of Henry Drummond's classic, *The Greatest Thing in the World*. It was a compact, pocket-sized edition. But it was destined by God to open my understanding of His purposes for me as no other work had ever done.*

It was said by D. L. Moody that in all his life he had never met a more honest, genuine, or Christlike man than Henry Drummond. Drummond was more than just a pastor. He was a highly esteemed scientist who wrote and spoke for the Most High in common layman's language.

His essays made an incredible impression on me. In part they generated deep within my soul an insatiable appetite for the very life and character of Christ Himself. If Drummond could know, love, and relish the company of Christ in his beloved Scottish hills, why could I not come to cherish Christ's companionship in the same manner out in the wild and untamed wilderness of British Columbia? I read and ruminated over what this hardy Scot had written until the books by him I had bought were almost worn out with wear. Their spines were broken; the pages were faded and torn, but their eternal truths were gems stored forever in the vault of my memory and soul.

Though Drummond died in his mid-forties of a dreadful disease that racked his whole body with appalling pain, the impact of his short sojourn here changed my own character forever. I never met the man. Yet in truth he remains as one of my dearest friends. Christ in His compassionate concern allowed my path to cross Drummond's upon the pages of his books. In Christ's gentle way, His gracious Spirit has used this author to draw me ever nearer to Him as my dearest Friend in all the world.

In plain but persuasive terms, Drummond quietly introduced me to Christ in a manner no one up until then had ever done. He literally led me gently to meet the Master in such a firsthand encounter that it shaped the entire countenance of my character for years to come. Though at that point in my spiritual pilgrimage I was a skeptical scientist, arrogant in thought and worldly wise in my own profession, Drummond made me see the folly of my false thinking. Then with profound conviction he helped me to humble my haughty heart before the Most High Majesty of the universe.

Down through the ensuing years, great and noble books written by great and noble men have enriched my entire life beyond my ability to describe. A number of these authors have become precious friends. Though I have never met them in person, and many have gone to be with the Lord, I turn to them often for insights from above. In honor, respect, and admiration I wish to name some of them here: Andrew Murray, Augustine, Oswald Chambers, Marten Lloyd Jones, Tozer, A. B. Simpson, Spurgeon, T. B. Maier, G. Campbell Morgan, C. S. Lewis, Watchman Nee, and D. L. Moody.

In actual, living reality these men have been used by our Father in the stillness of my own soul to mold my life more than any other influence. They themselves have become mentors to me. Out of the depths of their own lives, centered in Christ, they have drawn me to Him. They have opened up His supernatural revelation of Himself to me in terms I could understand and live by day after day.

They are authors, workers with God, who could so handle and explain His Word and His ways that His truth became to me spirit and life—life from above that permanently altered the contours of my character and conduct.

I am eternally indebted to these blessed friends. But I give even more genuine gratitude to God my Father for allowing me to be so enriched in coming to know Him firsthand through these friends. Like the woman at the well, who told her village about the Living Water, these authors have eagerly entreated me to come and meet the Master.

Now I in turn, out of a long and intimate communion with Him, endeavor to gently introduce my readers to Him. This matters most! It is the main motive for my life's work—that anyone who reads what I have written will discern, "This man knows God."

For some thirty-five years now, scores and scores of letters, cards, and messages of various kinds have come to me from all over the world. Many, many of them address me as a friend, as a guide, as one who has gently opened their comprehension to eternal truth. I have been moved mightily to hear how, because of my books, men and women have come to know, love, and trust Christ in wondrous ways.

This is in essence the supernatural work of His own gracious Spirit. It is a phenomenon of divine design that I am now considered a special friend to thousands upon thousands of precious people who have never seen my face nor even shaken my hand. I consider it a noble honor, one which our Father in His generosity has conferred upon this rough, old, mountain man.

And it matters much!

Because I have had to be sincere with my readers, I have had to be utterly honest and open with my dearest Friend, Christ.

It is not an easy thing to lay bare one's own soul and spirit before the harsh scrutiny of one's contemporaries.

But that is part of the price an authentic author must pay if his work is to move others to find life in Christ.

It must be done if He is to be honored.

And here I wish to reiterate once more that of all the books I own and cherish, by far the most precious is God's own revelation to us of Himself in His divine declaration. It is sometimes called the Holy Scriptures, or it is better known as the Book of the Law of God, more commonly called the Bible.

This collection of writings through which the Most High has disclosed His divine identity to us mortals is not a single volume. Rather, it is a miniature library of rare manuscripts in which our Father reveals not only His own character but also His conduct toward us. It is the most sacred of all scriptures revered by man, for the single, simple reason that God Himself is the author, not some human mind.

The Bible is the only book that adorns my desk. Visitors who come to our home are often curious to see where I work. They are utterly astonished to find a bare desk bearing only a simple table lamp, an old-fashioned fountain pen, and my well-worn Bible.

My Bible is the one Mother handed to me as a parting gift when I left home at eighteen to go overseas to study. In her magnificent wisdom she knew and prayed that this supernatural Word would become my guide and ground for godliness in a chaotic world. Her prayers and her desires have been honored by God.

That Bible is by far the most familiar book to me in all the world. It is so well worn that the back is broken, the pages are torn, the binding is frayed, the print is fading, almost every chapter is marked and underlined. In moments I can find any passage Christ brings to my attention.

It is my friend!

So much so that a few years ago when our cottage was threatened with a raging forest fire, friends asked me what I wanted to save most from the flames. My instant reply was, "My Bible." No other possession seemed to matter much in that horrendous hour. But my Bible would not be burned. It mattered most!

In a much broader sense, God's Word matters most in our world where so much is now awry. It is the only single, sure, unshakable security upon which any human society can construct an enduring civilization. At the turn of this century now coming to a close, when the might and influence of the British people dominated a quarter of the globe, they were known and called the people of the Book. In the great era of worldwide mission advances, the Bible was the secret of Britain's accomplishments under God's great hand. It ushered in the high noon of a society that honored God and quietly revered His Word.

But the last hundred years have seen a gangrene-like moral decadence consume our civilization. Men and women posing to be wise in their own ways have rejected God's Word. Humanism, atheism, communism, and a dozen other deceptive philosophies have turned the minds and hearts of the masses not only against God our Father, but also against Christ our Friend and Savior. They ridiculed and repudiated God's Word, which is supernatural life, then wondered why we are dying in unbridled violence, corruption, crime, and chaos.

I declare, without apology, that unless we turn back again to the Bible, the Book, we shall perish as a people. We shall collapse as a civilization. We shall be blown away into oblivion. God's divine declaration matters most in all things.

---

* Kregel Publications has just released a new, updated edition of this classic work. This new edition contains a helpful summary of Henry Drummond's influential ministry and a further expansion of his book by Lewis. A. Drummond.

CHAPTER FOURTEEN

The Acceptance of Adversity in Humility

In this book every effort has been made to portray those positive and powerful aspects of life that, when all is said and done, really matter most. So it is with reluctance that in this chapter the whole question of adversity is examined in honesty and humility. My earnest prayer and sincere hope is that the pages that follow will be used by our Father to encourage and energize the reader.

In contemporary English we use various euphemistic phrases to deal with our difficulties. We say,

"That is the way the cookie crumbles."

"Tough luck. You've been dealt a bad hand of cards."

"Life's like that. You can't win them all."

In more straightforward language, the basic concept being expressed is that adversity comes to us all. No human being is exempt from tough times. Christ Himself, who endured so much adversity, alerted us that we, too, as His people, must face trials.

Any preacher or any teacher who misleads people into believing that God's children will be free from trouble is a deceiver. It simply is not so! In fact, from cover to cover, God's divine revelation gives us accounts of men and women who faced adversity. In quiet humility and calm confidence these people accepted its onslaught with fortitude and unshakable faith in our Father's care. In the furnace of affliction they brought honor to the One who could sustain them there, and then, in His own good time, deliver them.

The ability to persevere with dignity and self-composure under God's great, good hand of blessing is of the utmost importance. It really does matter most.

There is no gain in trying to explain why trouble comes into our lives. It may surprise you that God's Spirit discloses to us that we are born into trouble, whether our days be many or few. We must accept it, overcome it, and so prevail in the energy of the Most High!

Adversity comes in many guises. It comes from many different directions and in unexpected ways. Perhaps most perplexing, it often comes at very inopportune moments in life. It takes us unaware. So we are often baffled and bewildered. A common response we make is "Why? Why does this happen to me just now?"

Thousands of sermons have been preached that try to answer that single, simple, searching cry of the human spirit. Almost as many books have been written, trying to analyze the dilemma and offer solutions. There is nothing to be gained here by delving into reasons for all of the pain, sorrow, suffering, reverses, and tragedy that comprise part of the tapestry of our few short years here.

I am writing to you now as an elderly man who, in the last half of his life, has honestly endeavored to walk in close and unclouded communion with Christ my Friend. After some thirty-five years of this intimate interaction with the Living God, I am firmly convinced that adversity in any form and from any quarter at any time is part and parcel of His arrangement of my affairs. It is permitted to impact my life in order to shape my own character, to alter my conduct, to deepen my faith and confidence in Christ's character and His wondrous commitments to me as His friend.

This means I can truly trust Him in any trouble!

I am fully aware that this may sound very pious on paper. The reader may even sneer inwardly, insisting that such a statement hardly cures the cancer, redeems a wayward child, or covers expenses when there is no job.

But I beg you to read on and hear me out. For the other alternative is to fret and fume over the misfortune and fight it in a frenzy of fear and foreboding. The struggle only makes the adversity grow ever greater in our estimation until it consumes us like a malignant and terminal cancer.

There are millions upon millions of human beings who, across the drastic drama of human history, refused to accept adversity in humility. They have railed against misfortune, heaped abuse upon it, and vented their anger against both God and man because of it.

It is not easy to tell people this; certainly it will not make me popular, but maybe it will save someone from awful self-destruction: Personal pride prevents most people from accepting adversity with humility.

Almost all of us, without exception, believe deep down that we deserve better. We are sure we are getting a "bum rap" from life. We tell ourselves the cards are stacked against us. So in anger, rage, bitterness, and hostility we lash out at the adversity.

Not only do these acid-like attitudes corrode our own characters, but they spill out of our antagonistic spirits to scald and burn others around us. All of which only adds to our trouble and darkens our days.

On the other hand, the person who accepts adversity in a quiet attitude of submission to our Father's arrangements becomes humble in heart. The fretting and fuming end. Peace prevails within, then hope runs anew on the horizon.

Acceptance really matters most in the anguish of adversity. It means one can find the consolation in our Father's care to carry on with calm confidence. There comes into the stress and strain of the soul that sublime assurance that our Father does all things well. Even in the most dire difficulties and in the most troubling times this is so!

There is no other greater secret to overcoming the attrition of adversity than what has been stated in the preceding paragraph. There is no other way to handle the disappointments, setbacks, and sorrow that assail us in life. Most troubles are not done in a day. They often dog our footsteps for years and years. They are not just a brief moment of anguish. They are more often a heavy burden that can be borne for years only with the calm confidence that Christ also bears them with us. So we can endure. So we can prevail. So we can praise Him and give true thanks even in trouble.

This is the path to peace.

This is the way to rest in Him.

This is to find power to overcome adversity.

It takes a humble heart, a contrite spirit, and a lowly attitude of mind to accept adversity from our Father. Most of us refuse to believe that, if He is indeed the God of love and compassion, He would ever allow adversity to assail us. This attitude toward Him demonstrates that we fail to understand His true character of love and His profound concern for His children.

This is best understood in the categorical statement made in the utmost clarity by His own gracious Spirit: "My son, despise not thou the chastening of the Lord, nor faint when thou art rebuked of him: For whom the Lord loveth he chasteneth, and scourgeth every son whom he receiveth" (Heb. 12:5–6).

Two horrendous experiences that have touched my own life speak eloquently in clarifying our Father's profound concern and care. Through them He has taught me what I have been trying to express in this chapter. Writing these accounts is not easy, for there is deep pain involved.

My first beloved life mate, Phyllis, and I were both forty-five years old when the cancer specialists told us she was stricken with the most virulent form of this dreadful disease. Already it had made massive inroads into her body.

The doctors were kind enough to call me in for a private consultation. They confidentially prepared me to face her imminent death. They warned me that the advance of the affliction simply could not be halted. And most terrible, not only would it consume her within, but it could be openly visible, destroying her beautiful body with its appalling corruption.

They tried to prepare me to face the formidable fact that science had absolutely no way to arrest this awful disease. The very best we could do was to take her home and there face the fury of the awful onslaught more or less on our own—but with help from our Father.

I do not intend to overwhelm the reader. Only those who have endured living with death month after month can begin to know the absolute agony and anguish of such an ordeal. The soft sobs muffled in the pillows night after night. The dreadful, appalling stench of putrefaction. The horror of huge, gaping areas of flesh destroyed, which we tried in vain to hide.

This was not an affliction one could face with pious platitudes or glib remarks about bearing our burdens bravely. With death on the doorstep, death in the bedroom, death destroying my beloved by degrees before my eyes, death laying waste a wonderful woman, death demolishing all the dreams we ever shared, we both needed more than any man, any pastor, any church, or any human sympathy could ever provide. We had to have the rock-solid assurance of our Father's presence with us in the pain. We had to know that this awful adversity, which lasted for over two years, was part of a greater plan for our good.

In the dreadful darkness of that long, endless night we would hold each other as close as we could and whisper softly, "Whom the Lord loveth He chastens!" We did this until the day she died in my arms, until the very moment invisible angels swept her away into glory, the great door to the room of death slamming shut behind them. In a bottomless pit of sorrow there was yet a stupendous assurance. She is free! She is free! Free at last from all of earth's agony! The anguish is over! She is home! She is at rest!

It took several years to fully accept this adversity. Little by little in the loneliness that pervaded my life, I began to see that our Father had done us both a great favor. Through the fire of this affliction He had drawn us to Him. He forged in our souls an unshakable faith in His care. He sustained us in strength and quietness that astonished all the doctors, nurses, and onlookers who watched us deal with death.

As the years advanced and our society rapidly became more rank, more raunchy, more reprobate, I realized Phyllis had been spared from terrible sorrow. Her sensitive spirit would have been wounded ten thousand times by the turmoil of our world. Our Father does all things well! When I, under His great hand of love, accept adversity in humility, I too find rest in Him.

The other instance that I wish to recount concerns one of my dearest and most cherished friends. He is now ninety-four years of age, still lively, still buoyant in His faith in Christ, still joyous in his contact with others, still a man our Father uses to inspire and enrich all of us. His has been the saga of His Master's servant, laying down his life gladly for the feeble and the forgotten all around him.

Yet, almost next door lives his only child, a son greatly cherished, a man well into his sixties who has never capitulated to Christ. In fact, he tends to scoff at the humble, quiet faith of his dad. He behaves as though it is absurd to trust in God at all. Much better to just be rough and tough making his own way through the tangles of life with his own wit and work.

How very often in my quiet moments of communion with Christ, there comes to my spirit something of the terrible suffering this dear old dad endures over his wayward son. This is not a fleeting affliction that lasts a few months. It is an ongoing anguish that has not diminished for nearly half a century!

Still this dear old saint of God accepts the adversity in grace and humility. He has died a thousand deaths over this stubborn son. Yet he pushes on, giving thanks to God for His bountiful blessings. Always, always his life, his letters, his laughter bubbles over with good cheer. Wherever he goes there flows from his soul a stream of spiritual refreshment to others.

What is his secret amid all his sorrow?

He accepts adversity with honest humility.

He gives God thanks even for this stress.

He knows our Father does all things well.

This is what matters most in tough times in tough places!

CHAPTER FIFTEEN

Forgiveness, Fairness, Firmness, Fun

Each of the above four topics could have an entire chapter devoted to it. But I have chosen to combine the four since each is so closely intertwined with the others. They are attitudes of life that matter most if we are to be joyous, cheerful, but effective people.

Forgiveness

All of us need forgiveness so desperately. All of us fail our Father God and we fail one another. This is why Christ, our Savior, our Friend, came to suffer in our stead, to atone for all our wrongs, to pay the supreme price with His own life laid down to secure our pardon.

Only on this basis of His own sovereign love for us could the supreme justice and absolute righteousness of God our Father be satisfied. It is on the basis of His own amazing grace and generosity, extended to us in complete forgiveness, that we are acquitted of our wrongs. Only on this basis can we enter freely, gladly into His family, fully accepted as His beloved children.

All of this He makes possible because He is our generous, compassionate, caring Father. This is why we can declare boldly without any doubt, "I have been forgiven," and cry out assuredly, "Oh, my God, You are my Father. Oh, Christ, You are my Savior, my Friend."

This is the titanic transaction that takes place within the soul and spirit of any person who quietly accepts Christ's complete pardon. His is a transforming power that sets a person free into a brand new dimension of life—a gracious, generous, forgiving life in which we are prepared to forgive others.

We love Him because He first loved us.

We forgive others because He first forgave us.

This forgiveness—which flows from the compassionate character of God Himself, extended to us in Christ, and confirmed within our spirits by His Holy Spirit—changes our very characters. We no longer demand an eye for an eye or a tooth for a tooth or a wrong for a wrong. We are actually re-created to the point where we extend forgiveness, pardon, and grace to others.

We become people who, in our daily deportment, show generosity, kindness, and forgiveness, just as Christ forgives us. It is a most joyous way to live. It delivers us from anger, inner hostility, bitterness, seeking revenge, and other atrocious attitudes that can otherwise bring so much darkness and despair within.

Show me the man or woman who is generous in forgiving others their faults and offenses, and I will show you someone who walks the high road of joy in company with Christ. There is an element of exhilaration, of enthusiasm, of divine energy clearly evident in the conduct of anyone who is forgiving.

Finally, in order to live a forgiving life, we must face the supreme fact that it is our Father who ultimately keeps all the accounts. It is He who has on file all the debts and all the little payments made in the push and pull of life. He knows exactly where we stand in settling the scores and unpaid debts that accrue to our accounts.

And the tough question each of us must ask ourselves hundreds of times is, Am I debt free? The simple answer to that short, stabbing query determines the degree to which I live in peace, good cheer, and contentment. It is impossible to know serenity of soul with the scourge of unforgiveness burning hot with revenge within. As God's forgiveness flows to me, it must also flow out to others.

Fairness

Freely I receive His gracious, generous forgiveness.

Then I for my part gladly pass on forgiveness.

There is no other way to be fair.

This balances the books.

It brings calm.

There simply is no other way to find serenity of spirit. This is the supreme secret to reducing the fret and fever of life. It is the path of peace on which we can walk with God in deep delight.

No old grudges.

No vicious vendettas.

No slow burning fuses of frustration.

No inner cancer of criticism and scorn.

Any one of them can destroy you from within. They can diminish any good you may attempt to do. They can ruin your peace of mind and wreck your entire outlook.

Clear the decks.

Be fair with others.

Remember each of us carries a load of care.

Put the best face on what others do or say.

Be bighearted, full of goodwill.

Look for some hint of wholeness in the man or woman who wrongs you.

After all, each of us, unwittingly, and in a careless moment, have brought grief.

We really do not need to fret, fume, and fight our way through life. It is possible, with God's gentle guidance, to take the high road of wholesome attitudes and quiet contentment in His company. Our few years here must be marked with gestures of help, hope, healthy goodwill, as we are fair with others. They will remember these gentle touches forever. And we will be blessed.

It never fails to astonish me how our Father always, always balances the books of life when we live openly, honestly this way. It is what He calls "walking in the light," before both Him and others. With no hidden grievances, no secret animosities, no rotten attitudes masked by a false front, we become just plain people, living simply in love and laughter that lightens the road others walk with us.

We are all pilgrims on that rocky road. We all have our tears and our triumphs. We all have our dark nights and shining days. Let's be fair and in quiet good cheer stretch out a hand or extend a smile to others who struggle on the same as we. We are all in this together.

I assure you no act of fairness or genuine compassion ever goes unnoticed. No simple gesture of goodwill is ever overlooked. No private deed of dedication passes unseen. God our Father is here. He is in every secret place. He prompts every good and generous action. He loves to pour out His benefits and His bounties on those who in turn pour them out to others.

He gives endlessly.

He shares limitlessly.

He loves boundlessly.

So to be fair, it follows that I do the same. Pass along the love, the laughter, the lightheartedness of His companionship to the weary ones, the woebegone. Be bold and brave in living gladly for God.

How else will the lost ever get a glimpse of God our Father unless they see something of His life in me? Jesus said plainly, without apology, "He that has seen Me has seen the Father!" So should it be with me.

Firmness

Coupled with our forgiveness of others, we need to demonstrate deep inner convictions in our lives and conduct. Our Father has not left us in doubt about proper and appropriate behavior, about what is right and what is wrong. His eternal verities shall endure forever. His laws cannot be violated without bringing most serious consequences on the offender. Not because He is harsh and hard, but simply because His divine ordinances are designed for our own good. When ignored and rejected with impunity, those principles for proper and prosperous well-being boomerang with dire consequences on the one who breaks them.

At the close of this century, our entire civilization, with its colossal chaos and confusion, with its mayhem and madness, with its crime and corruption, gives stern witness to a society that flouts our Father's clear instructions for human conduct. It is not the violation of our so-called "human values" or "family values" or "American values" that has led to so much violence. It is our disregard for our Father's loving values! Each designed for our supreme benefit and blessing.

His standards for human society matter most.

We are instructed to study them carefully, just as we would in learning the rules of the road for driving.

We are commanded clearly to comply with His gracious commands in our daily conduct.

We are assured over and over again that to do His bidding with goodwill is to be blessed.

Our obedience is not an adherence to harsh, hard legalism. Rather it is to show our love, loyalty, and glad submission to His sovereignty. We see it as an honor to be people under His command. We are firm in our faith and fidelity to His honor!

The tragic and terrible weakness of the contemporary church is that its people are not rock solid in their faith in the living Lord Jesus Christ. Their leaders are so eager to pack their sanctuaries with happy people, so keen to come to an easy accommodation with the world, so willing to be soft on sin and tolerant of almost any lifestyle, that the church has almost no impact on our culture.

If we are going to shape our society to serve God and honor Him, it will not be at the ballot box or through the political powers per se. It will be by the relentless power of God's own gracious Spirit becoming supremely in control of individual believers who are firm in their devotion to Christ. People, plain people who stand on their faith in our Father, will shape society and change our civilization for good more than will ten thousand, big-time TV campaigns with all their glitz and glamour.

God is not looking for smooth, slick communicators. He is looking for a few noble souls who will stand firm for Him, who will not flinch before their foes, who will not fear no matter how much others may rant and rave in rage. Let me name but a few of these dauntless ones:

Joseph in Egypt,
Daniel in Babylon,
Paul in Greece and Italy,
Augustine in Africa,
Florence Nightingale in the Crimea,
Wilberforce in Britain,
Abraham Lincoln in North America.
It takes courage to be firm and fearless.
It means a man or woman must be bold for God and His Word.
It demands that we be different from the crowd.
But our Father honors those who honor Him!

Fun

You might be startled that I inject the subject of fun into a discussion of such serious topics as forgiveness, fairness, and firmness. But fun is an integral ingredient of all that I have said here. Why? Because to live after the way of God has proven to be anything but dull. Quite the opposite! To be fair, to be forgiving and forgiven, to be firm in our commitments to the living God guarantees great challenges and the sheer excitement of sharing in noble adventures with Him.

Please do not misunderstand what has just been said.

I am not referring to cheap thrills. Nor am I suggesting that following Christ is fun and games in our decadent generation, though some churches try to attract crowds by using entertainment. Such devices, however, will not endure.

Christ calls us to be forgiving—not easy.

Christ constrains us to be fair—very difficult.

Christ commands us to be firm in faith in Him—we so often fail.

But in this high and noble calling He constantly challenges us to be of great, good cheer! He commands us to be strong and of great, good courage! He expects and knows that it is perfectly possible for us to be exuberant with joy in Him. All because He takes our ordinary little lives and with them He achieves extraordinary accomplishments.

We are on the cutting edge by sharing in His life. We rejoice in the dynamic of doing His will. We experience the sheer delight of Him pervading our days with great purpose.

We discover that none of this is what the world calls "foolish" in contempt. Nor is it some sort of lighthearted levity now so common in the church. Nor is it vanity or pride or phony pretence.

It is Christ in me . . . joy unspeakable . . . and pleasures forever in His presence—true, pure fun!

CHAPTER SIXTEEN

The Joy of Mobility in Many Ways

I have always been a free spirit. I grew up in a frontier environment where my early life was free and unfettered by social restrictions. So I do not mean a "free spirit" in the modern mode where young people rebel against authority, cast aside moral restraints, then indulge themselves in destructive lifestyles.

No, what I am saying is that in relative freedom I roamed the hills around my home, free as the wind. At dawn, when the rising sun cast a faint glow over the rugged rock escarpments on the eastern horizon, I was up, dressed, ready with rifle in hand to slip away in search of wild game.

I always went alone. I went unencumbered by excessive hunting gear. Nothing more than khaki shirt and shorts, sturdy bush boots, and six shells (cartridges) in the magazine of my beloved rifle. There might be a bit of dried biltong (jerky) in my back pocket to sustain my strength for hours of hard hiking.

I loved the life of the African bush. Somehow the great wide vistas, the great sweeping plains, the great stillness of daybreak, were the elixir of life. I needed this wild, untamed, unfettered mobility to become a rugged, self-reliant man. My whole makeup demanded the uninhibited joy of roaming at random, free as the wind.

If by chance the coarse cough of a leopard, the bark of a bushbuck, or the warning cry of a baboon broke the stillness—so much more the rising sense of excitement. I was on my own in the wilds and I loved every hour of the hunt!

This marvelous mobility became most precious to me. I asked no one's permission to go free. My dad and my mother were wise enough not to hamper my movements as a maturing youth. Deep down they understood that my unshackled spirit demanded the inspiration and exhilaration of mobility, of freedom from human restrictions, no matter what form they took.

I was at heart a loner.

I was calmly self-confident, but not cocky.

I was quietly self-reliant, able to fend for myself.

I was fond of taking risks, facing danger.

I was in every sense free of fear.

I was a man on the move.

This powerful, pulsing, private passion has never left me. It has, under our Father's gentle guidance, taken me on scores and scores of joyous adventures all over the earth. Nor have these expeditions been just for my own sake, but they have also served to benefit others as well. My sturdy legs have carried me across the tough terrain of some forty countries around the world. I have wandered far and free.

Often, often, I bow my head in honest humility and give genuine thanks for the sheer joy of my free mobility. Though much of my life has been marked by fragile health, still there has been sufficient stamina to live free and to keep active. I discipline myself to keep on the move, to take long tramps, to hike the hills, to climb the ridges, to roam free along the ocean edge.

Each of these small safaris has meant much to me. They really do matter most if I am to remain robust in health, strong in spirit to serve my Master and my generation.

Many are the times, when all alone out in the mountains or by the sea, that I have implored God my Father to take me home while I was still in full stride. To become an invalid, confined to a bed, or fettered to a wheelchair would be worse than death. I am a man born free in an untamed land, like my beloved Masai people of East Africa. Their warriors could never endure imprisonment. They simply languished and died with broken spirits the week they were put behind bars. For too long they had wandered free in the wind, a part of the wild, untamed terrain that was never insulted with a fence.

For me mobility represents freedom of the first order. No one dictates to me where I shall go, where I shall work, where I shall live, or how long I shall stay. I often remark forcefully to Ursula, my beloved wife and life companion, "Darling—I am a free man, only under Christ's command. I shall not fear!"

Of course, this does not guarantee that I am always popular with my contemporaries. To many, who would like to compress me into their civilized mold, I am an awkward misfit. There are many people so tamed, so strained, so corseted by their culture they know nothing of mobility either in body or mind or spirit. Their chief concern is to comply with the rigid rules and regulations imposed upon them by others.

Not so for me! It may sound a bit hard boiled, but often I say to people who are not satisfied with my rather carefree conduct, "I am too old, too rough, too tough for you to whipsaw me around! So just lay off my life!"

And they do!

They shake their heads and leave me to be free.

Much of my life has been spent in North America, in parts

of the western region that enjoy a degree of openness and freedom not common in the more congested areas of the East. It is still possible to find wilderness and great mountain ranges untamed by man. As a young person I reveled in the unrestricted sweep of the magnificent West Coast, the roaring rivers rushing to the sea, the shining snowfields of the mountain ranges, the brooding expanses of the open foothills, and I relished the freedom to roam at will under desert skies.

Of course, there were risks.

There were heart-pounding challenges on the trail.

There were moments of marvelous mobility, when I was alone on the mountain.

All of these adventures shaped my character. They disciplined my conduct. They embellished my conversations. My life has been a joyous adventure with God Himself. All of my horizons are broad, fresh, inviting. New days bring new ways. The zest of living sings in my soul, stirs my spirit, and brings smiles to my face. For I have been blessedly free!

Free from the tedium of the same stale schedule.

Free from the boredom of the same surroundings.

Free from the dull repetition of endless regulations.

In part, lack of freedom is the root problem that makes life for millions and millions of residents in great cities such an abomination. They are trapped in tunnels of concrete, steel, and glass. Every move they make is dictated by the mind-set of the masses. Every thought they think is molded by the media. They are not free people. They are slaves to a sordid society in a tension-ridden environment. It is no surprise that in the ghettos of our great metropolitan centers crime flourishes, prostitution permeates the population, and drugs are a way of life. If those of us with hearts of compassion cry out over such appalling conditions, just consider how our Father weeps over His world!

The reader may very well ask, "What has all of this got

to do with mobility?" The terrible truth is that millions and millions of human beings are literally trapped in these groaning cities. There is no escape for them. There is no other place to which they can move. They are born into bondage and the grinding, gruesome environment of broken homes, broken hopes. By the time they are teens they are streetwise petty criminals, struggling to survive. Are we then surprised that such a culture produces people of despair, anger, and cynicism in their appalling poverty?

The politicians and pundits of our society love to prattle on about upward mobility for the masses. The formidable fact is that there is no place for them to go. Apart from a tiny handful who by almost superhuman willpower and a helping hand break free from their bonds, the vast majority sink down in deepening despair.

I was one of those millions. In Vancouver, I was caught in crushing, desperate degradation. I would have succumbed to this dreadful environment but for the grace of God my Father shown to me by a devout, elderly Scottish widow and her family. They took me into their hearts and into their home when I came to that bustling city, not knowing a single soul there, virtually broke, and looking for work.

Oh yes, I know firsthand whereof I write! It is an enormous honor to be mobile and free. It matters much.

Those of us set free to follow Christ wherever He may lead us, often find He takes us into the cruel, crushing cities that corrupt our generation. He takes us there in our mobility to lift the fallen, to touch the wounded spirits, to bring some solace to those who suffer, to set the captives free. I have gone into cities all over the earth to tell others of the freedom that only our Friend and Savior can provide. That is why Ursula and I have been so deeply involved with rescue mission work. That is why I have been able to support those magnificent men and women who serve in the Salvation Army.

Our Father does not grant us mobility just to indulge our own selfish desires to visit lovely places or spend time in search of personal pleasure. Mobility is a treasured aspect of our daily lives, which can be used wisely to enrich both ourselves and others in many ways. In truth and in humility we need to ask the questions over and over, "Oh Father, where do you wish me to go today? Who do you want me to meet on the path of life? What do you intend for me to say to those along the way?"

Taken in this spirit, the joyous freedom to get around becomes somewhat of a sacred trust. Every day can be an opportunity to share a smile, to extend a helping hand, to bring a bit of brightness into someone's tedious life, to inject a note of good cheer into the weary old world most people inhabit.

For me to live this way in sincerity and goodwill is much more important than having any so-called ministry.

Jesus Himself was a mobile messenger, and He quietly declared that His meat, i.e., His very life, His strength of purpose, was simply to do the will of His Father who sent Him into the world, and to finish His work (John 4:34).

The Master said this to His men, after He had paused to visit with the woman at the well. His brief chat with her changed her character and changed her community. It was not something staged, spectacular, or sensational. He came with gracious goodwill to a woman trapped in the tedium of her jaded life in a run-down town.

This is what mattered most to Him and to her.

It should also be what matters most to me!

In my mobility others should meet my Master.

One great obstacle often prevents many people from having mobility. It will not make me popular to raise the subject here, but to be honest and honorable I must. It could change your whole life with Christ if you will be open-minded and receptive to this salient truth: The vast majority of God's people have never, ever, been fully set free from their own possessions. They are, in fact, fettered to their families, their friends, their familiar surroundings, their own hearth and home, their own favorite pastimes, their own careers or self-chosen interests. The drastic truth is they are bound by their own belongings. They are preoccupied with serving and sustaining their own interests. They are, in fact, possessed by their possessions.

The net result is they never are free to follow Christ in glad abandon. They will not move under the impulse of His love and compassion. They refuse to budge to help heal a broken world. They simply are not available to His purposes. All because they have not been brave enough to be mobile and ready to respond to Christ's compelling call.

But for the few who do, life with Him erupts into a journey of joy. New horizons, new endeavors, new challenges, new adventures dot the way. He brings deep delight to any person prepared to part with their possessions and start moving with Him!

CHAPTER SEVENTEEN

Simplicity of Life—
Zest in Loving Others

A grand old veteran missionary said to me years ago, "Learn to travel light through life. Don't accumulate too much stuff!" This is sound and sensible spiritual truth.

If a person is determined, under our Father's gentle guidance, to be mobile, free, and available to His great, good purposes, then life needs to be reasonably free of encumbrances. For there is a sense in which a person really can struggle and expend an enormous amount of energy not only in caring for their belongings, but even more so in moving them.

About a year ago, an elderly man and his wife who felt God was calling them to a remote mountain community asked me to pray diligently for them. They hoped to start a little church in this frontier settlement and so decided to move all their belongings over there.

They lived about fifty miles from my home, so I could not see exactly what this move involved. Apparently the old gentleman was determined to make the move all on his own using his pickup truck. Every few days he would call on the phone to report his progress and ask for more prayer.

During one phone call, I was utterly astonished to hear that he had already hauled eighteen loads of stuff across the mountains and there was still more to go. Quietly I suggested that this would be a good time to give a lot of it away: share it with poor people; send some to the Salvation Army to help some struggling street people; give a few truckloads to the goodwill shops who would be glad to get anything of value for the approaching winter.

But the dear old fellow was loathe to part with his possessions.

As I reflected on the obvious stress and strain imposed on this couple by their belongings, I could not help but recall the incredible mobility of the Masai people among whom I lived and worked as a young man in East Africa.

They were a pastoral people, owning substantial herds of cattle, sheep, and goats. They were essentially nomads who moved often from place to place in search of fresh grazing and water supplies for their livestock. They were people on the move!

It never failed to astonish me how few their belongings were. All of their personal possessions could be easily loaded on the bony backs of a couple of donkeys, then they were off and away across the hills and plains of their vast grazing grounds.

They were an exceedingly cheerful people, full of great goodwill, enormous love and affection for each other, and deeply contented with life. In large part this was because they had mastered the art of simplicity. So that in the most practical ways possible they could give much of their time, thought, love, and attention to one another.

It always touched me deeply to see the quiet dignity and obvious respect with which they greeted each other. It moved me mightily to see how much time they took to engage in deep discussions and happy conversations with one another. In short, they really had time, and they took the trouble to spend it with each other.

This bonding of affection and devotion meant that their social fabric was tightly woven. Children were gifts, deeply treasured by all the tribe. There was no such tragedy among them as an "unwanted child."

How often I wished I had been born a Masai, not only for the simplicity of their life, but also for the sincere expression of their love for each other.

It surprised me to see how they extended their care and concern to our family when we came among them as newcomers. We came from a different culture, a different civilization, and were of a different color. Yet in grace and generous goodwill they took us to themselves in gentle gestures of love and concern.

The older men would come up to our place on purpose, just out of courtesy, to sit with me in the cool shade of the pepper trees. We would spend long sessions in lighthearted discussions about their cattle, the grazing, the weather, and our Father's care for us all.

The women and the girls would come almost every day to chat with my wife about our children and their children. They would come bearing little gifts of goodwill, which in turn were reciprocated by us. There was ample time to visit, to laugh together, and on occasion to cry together.

If one of their people was injured or mauled by a lion or leopard we did what we could to render first aid. We would often gladly haul them across the country to the nearest hospital some twenty-seven miles away.

We lived among the Masai during the awful time of the Mau Mau terrorists. In their concern for us, the Masai in great generosity offered to send a small contingent of their own armed warriors to sleep at our place and guard our home. You may be sure that gesture endeared these people to me in a wondrous way.

Why do I bother to recite these events, which took place so long ago? Because it was then I began to ask some very hard questions about life: What really matters most? What truly counts in the long run? What actually deserves most of my time and attention? Is it to be my personal possessions, or people?

I was very, very ill in those days. Night after night the pain was so severe, so acute, it seemed my end was near. The finest physicians in Nairobi seemed unable to diagnose my condition. In fact, one dear old, grey-haired doctor solemnly warned me that my end was imminent. The very best advice he could give me was to get out of the tropics at once.

At times like that, with death on the doorstep, what possessions one has seem of very little importance indeed. You surely cannot take them with you when you depart this life. So better to strip yourself down to the bare essentials if you expect the call home at any hour.

So in essence, my own personal view on living a very simple life was shaped some forty years ago out on the sweeping plains of the Masai in East Africa. If these noble people could live in quiet contentment and exuberant joy with so little, then so could I! It was not essential for me to gather up a bunch of unnecessary baggage and belongings to enjoy living. I learned how to travel light, ready to pack up and move swiftly at Christ's command.

I dared not let myself become cramped and constricted by the accoutrements of our Western world. I am, therefore, set free in a rather unusual way. I can live frugally and efficiently. I can find time and energy to share with others in need.

I am fully aware that my personal lifestyle of quiet simplicity without show or pretence poses problems for many in our complex Western world. They regard me as "odd," "unusual," even "a little off." But be that as it may, my approach to life can best be explained by a slogan I saw stuck on the back of a van parked next to us one day: "We live simply so that others may simply live."

If anyone comes into our home and happens to remark that they could use some article in our place, very often I pick it up and give it to them. It may be a piece of furniture, a book, some ornament on the wall, an article of clothing, a tool. It doesn't matter, it is gladly passed on to someone who can put it to good use.

Not only is the recipient pleased with the new possession, but I am glad to be of some help. The side benefit is that very, very few things accumulate around me. The decks, so to speak, are always cleared for action. There are few obstacles to get in the way.

Not long ago, one of my publishers was shocked to find out that I did not own a fax machine. When I informed him that I did not even own a word processor, a Xerox copier, or any other high-tech equipment of this century, it was assumed I had really lost touch. But the truth is the opposite. For my life is not complicated. I simply, steadily, get on with the work that my Father day by day entrusts to me. Without all the gadgets to complicate my life, it is simple to just get on with the job at hand.

Because I have been a serious writer for well over fifty years, most people assume I own a large and expensive library. I do not, simply because books are easy to accumulate, difficult to shelve properly, and very expensive to move. Long, long ago I learned that boxes of books are very heavy and terribly hard on a bad back.

I have had friends who owned impressive libraries. One of them boasted to me that he had more than four thousand volumes in his collection. Quite obviously he must never have read many of them. So what is the point in filling bookshelves with thousands of books that only gather dust? By diligent effort I have limited my library to about three hundred choice volumes. Each of which has been read and reread with unflagging interest. Many have become special "friends" across the years. And many of them I can share with others.

In the entire area of eating, drinking, and dressing, I have made a sincere endeavor to comply with Christ's commands. He indeed had our best interests in mind when he urged us not to give undue time and thought to food, drink, or clothing. Not that one has to exist on a spartan diet, but most North Americans are infatuated with food, drink, and the latest fashions. Of course this is in part because of the formidable barrage of advertising.

In our home we try intelligently to resist the trends toward fancy food and elaborate clothing. Our diet is quite frugal, mostly fruit and fresh vegetables for health. We seldom squander money eating out. And for the most part our wardrobe consists of a minimal amount of basic clothing. Why have closets cluttered with clothes that are not used?

Ursula and I are not ashamed to purchase what we need at sales. We have a sort of secret pact between us that we often refer to as fun: Because we save this way, we always have something to share with others who come to us in need.

As I see it, the chance to help the poor and needy comes only to those of us who have something to share. We need to understand that life with Christ calls for self-denial. It calls for self-discipline. It calls for managing whatever resources He entrusts to our care, so that we can in turn share His benefits with others. And the eternal, divine principle that He has ordained for us is simply this: The more we give away to others, the more he will bountifully bestow on us.

This idea of living quietly, calmly, with dignity and simplicity of life does not appeal to many people. They much prefer to live it up, to live lavishly, to impress others even if it means being deeply in debt. The inescapable reasons for this rather flamboyant lifestyle so common in our culture will be dealt with later, when we take up the matter of money.

Long ago I learned this basic truth: A simple life without fanfare or ostentation could be used by God my Father to benefit not only me, but also those in need who cross my path. He could and He does take my little loaves and my small fishes to feed, nourish, and sustain thousands of others, some of whom are far away but not beyond His reach.

My part is to live in simplicity, not cluttered with debt or defaults. To live free of encumbrances. To live ready, willing, and able to move for the Master at a moment's notice. This matters most if I am to be free to follow Him.

CHAPTER EIGHTEEN

Prayer for the Common Man—an Honor!

What is written in this chapter will not be understood by those who have not come to know Christ firsthand. Much of it may seem somewhat mysterious. And so it is, for it has to do with the inner life of the soul in contact with the living Christ.

But for me, a common man who on the common road of life communes quietly with his Father, prayer is of enormous consequence. It is a remarkable honor bestowed upon this ordinary human being who endeavors to cultivate and enjoy the presence of the living God.

At heart, prayer is being in the presence of God. It is being acutely aware that, "Oh Most High, You are here!" It is amazing how this assurance alters all of life. No longer is the world a rough, tough environment in which I struggle feverishly to survive the assaults of adversity and suffering.

The world instead becomes a sacred spot where I can live in quietness because His presence with me dispels the danger and calms my apprehension. All of this may sound somewhat mystical. Yet it need not be, for in an instant of intense prayer the soul can sense and know His peace.

Over and over our Father invites us to turn to Him. He urges us to come to Him for encouragement. He calls us to step aside softly into His company. He wants us to walk with Him, to talk with Him, to rest our souls in Him.

He actually finds great delight when His children draw near to Him in this way. He longs for our companionship. Not only does He want to hear us speak to Him, He in turn yearns to speak softly to us.

In essence this is prayer. It is also praise. Most important it is cultivating the precious presence of God our Father and the profound peace that His Son, our Savior and Friend, imparts to us within the inner sanctum of our souls and spirits. It is in the time of prayer that God's own gracious Spirit makes Christ very near and dear to us. He assures us and reassures us that all is well because He is here to reside with us in living reality.

Just recently, a younger couple came over to share an evening meal. After dinner our conversation turned to how we should spend our lives in God's company. It was a most stimulating discussion. Both of them had expressed the sentiment that their own lives were rather empty and devoid of meaning in our mad and hectic world.

They seemed to be under the impression that one had to have a "special ministry" in order to serve Christ, that somehow one had to do something sensational or spectacular to serve Christ and a perishing world.

It astonished them to no end when I said that Christ does not call us to be greatly successful, but He does call us to be quietly faithful. He does not expect us to be flamboyant, but He does expect us to be fruitful in good works. He does not call us to be high-profile public figures, but He does invite us to be humble enough to serve our generation in quiet goodwill.

None of this is possible if we prefer to be high-powered performers who try to impress others with our prestige. Our Father loves to draw near and share intimate moments with the man or woman who is humble in heart, and truly contrite in spirit!

This only happens when we deliberately take the time and thought and personal attention to pray in humble honesty throughout the day and night. It is this honest determination to spend time in calm communion with Christ that prepares our souls to receive Him as heaven's royalty.

He is the Almighty One who supplies our strength.

He is the Beloved One who arouses our loyal love.

He is the Faithful One who ignites our faith.

He is the Princely One who speaks peace to our souls.

So it is that when I engage in even the most ordinary work in the world and He shares in the endeavor, it takes on a divine dimension. It is He who brings enormous dignity, worth, and purpose to any work He gives me to do.

I explained to my friends that night how Christ calls each of us to serve Him steadfastly in our common lives. The work He gives me to do is seldom, if ever, seen by another soul. Morning after morning, week after week, month after month, I am up long before dawn, alone at my desk, being led gently by His Spirit to compose another manuscript.

There is no one else present to applaud my efforts.

There is no one else there to urge me on.

There is no one else at hand to help.

It is only He and I!

Yet at the same time I am excruciatingly aware that every thought that He brings to my mind, every impulse that stirs my spirit, every word I write is under His intense scrutiny. He and I are, in truth, coworkers in the endeavor He entrusts to me. This profound sense of His presence brings enormous delight into my daily duties.

My plain, simple, uncluttered work desk becomes a

sacred spot shared by Him and me. It will never, ever impress anyone else. Perhaps because it is so very plain, others would scoff in open disdain. But for me as a common man, it is here that day after day, and night after night, I commune with God my Father in honest prayer and humble praise. For it is an immense honor to have Him share His life with me so freely, so fully.

This matters most to me.

It is the precious presence of My Father in the hours we spend together that quicken my spirit to push on . . . even into my twilight years. It is His remarkable response to my uncomplicated, childlike petitions that is so profound. It is the amazing manner in which He speaks so clearly that gives the guidance I need to walk calmly with Him in a chaotic world.

Often, often I come to Him with open face, eager heart, and waiting spirit, asking for humility to walk with Him in His way. I never know what a day will hold, either of sunshine or storm. Only with Him holding my hand in His great but gentle grip can I hope to tread this path in peace.

The world through which I must walk has become so crude, so cruel, so crass, I need His perspective to prevail! I need to see others as He sees them, with eyes of compassion and care and sensitivity to their sorrows! I need to be reminded again, and again, and yet again that it is a noble honor to walk with Him in close communion.

He, and only He, can prevail on this common man to be always open and available to His best purposes. Only He can arouse my deepest devotion to His own fathomless love and grace.

Precious as prayer may be in my private relationship with my Father, it also has been given as a sacred trust to be used on behalf of others. When the mantle of entreaty is thus spread wider, prayer accomplishes God's purpose through the earnest petitions of His own humble people.

It continually astonishes me how alert and very responsive our Father is to the pleas of His own children, especially when spoken in the utmost sincerity. In part, of course, this is because He is here with us and knows our needs—even before we ask. But beyond that it is His remarkable generosity at work in granting our petitions when uttered in accord with His will and spoken in the authority of Christ's majestic name.

Across the long years of my own earthly pilgrimage with Him it has been moving for me, as a common man, to see God move on the landscape of my life. Always, always He is at work both in highly visible ways as well as behind the scenes, arranging my affairs in His delightful ways.

This arouses within my innermost being an irrepressible upwelling of praise, gratitude, and profound thanks to Him. Especially in my hours of quiet communion with Christ there flows forth rushing rivers of thanksgiving for all of His favors.

It is no small thing to be able to see Him change people, change character, change circumstances, change churches and leaders and communities. Not because any one of us is a remarkable person of prayer, but rather because He is, in truth, ruler of both heaven and earth. He holds all ultimate power in the universe. He, and He alone, will have the last word. He is God!

My part as a common man is to come into His royal presence in the utmost humility. Yet I come gladly for He is, in wonder and love, also my Father. So I come in calm confidence. He expects me to come with a pure heart of pure intentions. That is to say, He looks for a will, my will, set and determined to do His will without duplicity or pious pretence.

In short, what He wants is heartfelt honesty.

Never, ever, has He spurned an earnest prayer.

That prayer may be no more than a profound inner longing of soul, but it will be heard.

All because He knows the innermost intent of my soul and of my spirit.

He loves to hear me.

He loves to reply!

The manner in which our Father chooses to reward the prayers of His people may at times seem perplexing. There are those occasions in which He appears to act at once on our behalf. And so we are naturally elated. There are other times when He decides to do things quite differently than we expect. Then we often discover that He has accomplished much more than we ever anticipated. So we are surprised and overjoyed.

But then there are those trying circumstances that, from our human perspective, never seem to end, change very little, and almost seem to mock us. It is just here that we must ask for a double portion of grace to accept the long delay. We must ask for formidable faith to approve of our Father's arrangements. We must learn to rest quietly in absolute assurance of our Father's profound faithfulness. He will not fail us! He does all things well!

To live in this way with peace and contentment is not easy. It is, nonetheless, the honorable way to live, which brings enormous pleasure and satisfaction to our Father. For it means He has found children of His own who truly trust Him. He has the sweet companionship of those who rest in Him and delight in His care. And we in turn are rewarded and blessed by our childlike trust!

Perhaps the reader feels I have oversimplified the role of prayer in the life of God's child. I trust not. Quite the opposite, I have honestly attempted to emphasize that prayer is a high honor for any person who chooses to walk with God. It is an aspect of my life with Him that matters most.

There is a final dimension to my prayers as a common man, which I mention here in great earnestness. Namely, how Christ Himself can accomplish so much if we will just trust Him to do His great work in the world. With the explosion of modern technology, the incredible increase of information, the colossal capacity for mass communication, the church is sometimes tempted to do God's work, but in the ways of the world. To imagine we can do this is both a delusion and a deception.

Our Father still calls His children to rely on Him to accomplish His own good purposes on the planet. He calls us to place our confidence in Him and in His Word. He calls us to pray that His will, His work, His way will prevail in the earth.

The clear, categorical injunction given to us states, "Your faith should not stand in the wisdom of man, but it should stand in the power of God."

And that is possible for this common man, only if in honest prayer he trusts his Father God to do all things well . . . always.

CHAPTER NINETEEN

Serving as God's Steward

This may very well be the most difficult chapter in this book for me to compose in simple terms. For in large part it flies in the face of all the basic financial concepts that dominate the Western world. People, both secular and sacred, are so deeply immersed in the accumulation and use of money that the precepts stated here are often ridiculed and actually despised as being unworkable.

Still I have prayed earnestly that God's own gentle Spirit will guide me clearly in declaring how to handle our money to honor our Father and enrich others. For whether we like it or not, we live in a materialistic world. And surrounded as we are by so much that deceives and seduces us, we need divine direction in being responsible stewards in using and sharing the resources entrusted to us.

First, it should be said that the acquisition of wealth is absolutely no guarantee of joy or contentment. Very often the exact opposite is the case. I have worked closely with some of the wealthiest individuals both in the U.S.A. and Canada. It always astonished me to see the high level of their personal discontent, coupled with a deep fear of losing what they had already accumulated.

Secondly, it is an irrevocable fact that there is "never

enough." A peculiar, perverted dissatisfaction drives people to pile up more and more. One million dollars will not do. There has to be at least two. And in turn that has to be increased. The drive goes on and on. One must have more and more.

Our Master held all of this up to ridicule when He declared in Luke 12:15 that man's life does not consist in the abundance of what he possesses. But our secular society is completely convinced that material wealth is the true measure of our success and our security. Even in the church, many leaders say this is so.

Thirdly, all of us, unless truly enlightened to the truth by God's Spirit, are sure we actually own what we possess. Allow me to be very direct. When we were born we brought nothing with us into the world. And when we die we depart, leaving all material things behind. So it follows that at best a human being only holds in trust what he or she has for a few years. In other words, each of us is really not an owner but a steward.

Fourthly, there is abroad in our culture the false concept that a person can protect their possessions. All sorts of elaborate and complicated schemes are set up to secure personal wealth. There are innumerable investment strategies. There are endless financial devices designed to safeguard wealth. Yet, amazingly, the best of them fail. Fortunes are lost. And in the chaos of our culture most estates are utterly laid waste within three generations.

Despite all of these grim facts, most people still insist in trying to "pile it up." They sweat and struggle and scheme to attain this ever elusive success. Money and means and material wealth become their main preoccupation. They talk about it. They think about it. They work for it. They give themselves to it.

The result is far too many people are actually enslaved to the financial affairs of life. Their chief preoccupation is involved with paying off their bills, meeting their financial obligations, and forever trying to discharge their debts.

Because of all this, many well-meaning individuals are caught in a web of debt with many strands to it. They have been seduced by the lie that easy credit, low-cost loans, and borrowing beyond their ability to pay is a shortcut to prosperity. For multitudes it means instead a grim struggle just to keep ahead of their creditors.

Sad to say, this struggle is a reality for many of God's children. Instead of being debt free, with means at their disposal to help others in distress, they become mired in the mud of financial despair.

This is a terrible trap to be in. Like a fly drawn to the shining, silvery strands of a spider's web, so the unexpecting are drawn to the glamour and glitter and greed of our seductive society. Advertising and subtle salesmanship convince consumers they must have the brightest and best. Strong appeals are made to our human vanity, pride, and folly. So we fall for the deception, not realizing that things or money or so-called success cannot satisfy the deep longings of the soul and spirit that long for God Himself.

Because I have written at great length in other books of my own inner struggle with these issues, I shall not enlarge on them here. However, the burning question remains: How shall I serve my generation as God's servant, as his steward? Put plainly, How can I help others in a practical way? For all around us everywhere, all over the earth, we have poor people, perishing people, for whom our Father has enormous compassion, and so should we.

What follows are some profound principles of God's design, which can enable us to bless others if we will follow them. I shall endeavor to explain them in very simple terms. They may well serve to set someone free from their deception by the world.

(1) There is no such thing as a self-made person. To even think so is false and foolish pride. It denies God our Father

His dues. It is He who has endowed us with every capacity we have, whether it be to think, to reason, to learn, to speak, to work, to gain power, to influence others, or to acquire any wealth. Each is a gift to us out of His generosity.

(2) We are not our own. We are His children. We belong to Him. He created us. He sustains us. He cares for us. He accepts us as His own. He enfolds us in His family. So we are not free to "strut our stuff" or goof-off in vanity or pride, pretending to be masters of our own destiny.

(3) He, and only He, who has given us His Son as our Savior, Redeemer, and Friend, can set us free from slavery to our selfish interests. Only He can set us free from the folly and futility of sin. Only He can set us free from the subtle snares and lies of Satan the deceiver, who would destroy us.

(4) The living Lord Jesus Christ extends to us His own supernatural life. So we are now free to follow Him, free to carry out His wishes, free to turn away from all the false concepts of a fallen world. We are set free from the delusions and deceptions of a debt-ridden society.

(5) He has given us all things freely. In turn all He asks is that we pass them on freely to others. The more we give away, the more He gives us to share. We cannot "out-give" God, for His very makeup is to give and give. So He in turn is delighted to see us become cheerful, glad-hearted givers!

(6) When He sees that we can be entrusted with small benefits that we pass on to bless others, He will soon increase our resources. If we are faithful custodians of a few gifts, very quickly He will entrust more and more to our care.

(7) Just as our Father sent His Son into the world to give unceasingly of Himself, so now Christ commissions us to serve the world by generously giving of all that we are entrusted with by Him. In truth, all that we have during our few years here is actually held in trust. We are His stewards for a suffering generation.

If in fact these seven tenets form the foundation of our

life with Christ, then we see in brilliant clarity that we are called to serve. We are challenged to be faithful stewards. We are honored to be Christ's coworkers in a chaotic century. We are among those chosen to bring hope, health, healing, and help to a broken world.

As I have said scores and scores of times to hundreds of listeners, "God our Father can use the most ordinary person to accomplish the most extraordinary purposes, if that person is willing to do God's bidding. Not because we are great people, but because He is our great God!" That is the supreme secret in being a faithful steward.

This truly is one of those things that matters most in life. Does my willingness to help others lift their load, reduce the grinding pressure of poverty, bring health and healing to the stricken, shine new hope into hearts dark with despair?

These are legitimate questions. They demand honest answers. It is not enough for us to shrug them aside as if these were the duties of the Salvation Army, rescue missions, or humanitarian relief organizations.

Our Father constantly brings poor, unfortunate, weary people across our paths. It is not enough to merely pretend piety and in reality remain untouched by the weight of others' infirmities, to be people who do no more than pray, who are not prepared to live quiet, frugal lives so we have the wherewithal to provide others with food, clothing, and care.

It takes time. It takes thought. It takes effort. It takes money and resources we would otherwise spend on ourselves to help redeem a broken, battered world, rife with grief, loneliness, and remorse.

Just a while ago, I felt constrained by Christ to visit an elderly man whose beloved wife passed away. The first rainy day I came to his house the whole yard was in absolute chaos. Nothing seemed to have been tended for a very long time. I knocked on the battered door, but no one was home. I turned away with deep wounds within. I picked up his fallen fruit.

A week later I was back again. The front door was ajar, so I knew he must be home. I shouted and shouted to get the old gent's attention. Finally I heard heavy footsteps. He came clumping to the door with huge, mud-splattered boots reaching up to his knees. His clothes were disheveled as he waved me into the house.

It was as if a tornado had torn the place apart. Old newspapers, empty shopping bags, and trash were strewn about. Garden tools were lying on chairs, and everywhere there was the air of despair. It was not the time to turn away from this lonely heart, so grieved, so heavy.

It was not food, or clothing, or shelter the old gentleman needed that dark and cloudy morning. It was simply old-fashioned company. It was just a bit of time and fun and laughter to lift his spirits. It was someone to share a bit of joy.

I came away with the clear impression that this had been a morning well spent in bringing hope, smiles, and good cheer to a sad soul. As I see it, that is stewardship in the rough and tumble of a troubled world.

Often, often I am deeply moved when others in turn reach out to touch my life with winsome acts of love. One day, when Ursula was away for several weeks, an elderly couple called to see if they could come over and share the evening with me. I was elated.

Not only did they have to drive more than ten miles through difficult terrain, but the dear folks came bearing a delicious dinner of piping hot, home-cooked dishes. I was absolutely amazed at their generosity.

As if in celebration, we set the dinner table with shining silver and our finest dishes. We even lit a pair of candles to soften the scene. Then, in the gentle glow of each other's companionship, we shared an evening of goodwill that lingers on as a fond memory.

Those dear, simple, precious people had been such good stewards of their time and love and care. Blessings!

CHAPTER TWENTY

Courage to Carry On

As we move gently but steadily down the path of life toward the setting sun, perhaps one thing we seek most earnestly from our Father is just the courage to carry on. In saying this I am not referring to the basic fortitude all of us require to overcome the adversities of advanced age. Rather, I speak of the special courage necessary to continue to serve Christ and to minister faithfully to those whom He brings across our paths.

To be good stewards demands much more than just dawdling our days away in pleasure-seeking. It calls for courage of a very high caliber to carry out Christ's commands in a society that is steadily degenerating into decadence. It is a matter of being both brave and bold for our Father in a world where right behavior is increasingly ridiculed and crude conduct is applauded.

Simply put, it calls for immense courage of character to dare to be different. The more so during that interval in life when one's physical strength diminishes, and it is tempting indeed to sit back and let the world go to the dogs of despair.

When Christ moved among us in human guise, He spoke emphatically about the need for us to be faithful and

147

steadfast to the end. By the "end" He was obviously speaking of the end of each person's private pilgrimage upon the planet. Steadfastness is not always easy, for one must have fortitude of faith in our Father.

I give it as my personal testimony that no other single duty commands more of my close and constant communion with Him. Again and again I give hearty thanks for His remarkable faithfulness to me, but in the same breath beseech Him for courage to carry on!

And this courage matters most to me as an elderly gentleman. Over and over in His interaction with me I am astonished how often He urges me to be strong and of great courage. He instructs me to be brave and bold. He commands me to be a man of good cheer. He asserts that I am expected to be unafraid and fearless in this fear-ridden world.

He is not expecting the impossible of me. He does not demand conduct beyond my capacity. He does not mock me! What then is the simple secret to strength, serenity, and surety in a culture shot through with confusion and chaos? Whence comes the calm courage to carry on bravely as His person in the midst of such mayhem? How does one nourish formidable faith that will not be shifted from its foundation in our Father's character?

These are pressing questions.

They demand clear answers.

We must know how to endure to the end.

What are serious thinkers going to do with Hebrews 11:36–40?

What about the Mau Mau terrorists in Kenya?

What about the oppression of Islamic regimes?

What about the slave camps of Siberia?

What about the catacombs of Rome?

All these called for courage to carry on!

Just yesterday the following statement was flashed in large, bold letters on the television screen. This was not a speech from a spokesperson trying hard to impress an audience. It was a plain, simple, telling assessment of our society. It was not on a religious program.

Pause and reflect!

"Out of all the civilized nations on earth, the United States of America has by far the highest crime rate, the most violence, and increasing corruption."

That is a shocking but true statement.

It is high time serious-minded people face the facts.

No longer can North Americans, whether in the United States, Canada, or Mexico, claim to be so civilized.

We cannot boast blatantly about being "the best" countries in the world.

We must stop kidding ourselves about how very smart and sophisticated we are. It is a lie!

This applies to both Christians and non-Christians. We are residents in a decadent and cruel culture. We have so corrupted and contaminated our social and our biological environment that it has become a dangerous place in which to live. And it will not be improved by lame attempts to gloss over our greed, our self-centeredness, and our sins.

So we return to the basic, searching, sobering question: How can one be brave enough and bold enough to meet the challenge of this degradation with courage?

That fortitude can only be found in the very character of God our Father. It is undergirded in the eternal truths of His own commitments to us as His children. He fulfills them for us, in us, through us by example of His own impeccable conduct, which assures us that He is totally trustworthy. Nowhere else in all the world is there such assurance.

Just recently, I sat engrossed in deep conversation with one of the finest minds I have ever met. The man is very elderly, very experienced, very intelligent. With eyes growing dim, furrowed brow, and low tones he told me how, in the heyday of his youth and mid-life strength, he had unshakable confidence in liberal views. He was sure the high-sounding schemes of radical socialism and the sweet reason of humanistic philosophies would provide the panacea for the world's social problems. But they simply had not worked. Now in old age, at the end of his life, he looked out in dismay and despair on collapsing civilizations rife with cruelty and corruption.

"What went wrong?" he asked in sorrow.

My reply was very brief, very direct, very clear. "It is that men in their pride and intellectual arrogance have rejected the eternal God and His unchangeable truths. The end result is chaos and confusion!"

He was very quiet, very still, very reflective. It was a tense moment in time, in eternity, for both of us. It had called for courage to be so bold with a newfound friend. I wondered if in fact it might end our cordial comradeship.

Happily not so! For I met him again as he came back from a long walk in the spring sunshine. He warmly placed his long, bony arm around my shoulder. He hugged me gently. And I knew then the day was drawing near when I could gently, calmly introduce him to my Friend and Savior, Christ Himself.

All of this may sound so easy.

But really it is not, for you see, he is a Jewish gentleman!

He has been in the forefront of social change in a far-off country. But now our Father is drawing him into His own dear family.

There is a second dimension to life during the twilight years that calls for calm courage just to carry on. It is the relentless attrition of death in your circle of friends and associates. This is particularly true if your own life is extended while those around you are cut off at a younger age. Strange as it may seem, this was an anguish for which no one had prepared me.

In part this may be because my parents both died at a

relatively young age. Furthermore, I did not have any surviving siblings. Consequently, it has come as a subtle form of unexpected stress to lose fifty-seven dear friends during the past few years.

Their loss represents a huge tear in the fabric of my life. It means that those whom I turned to so often for encouragement, companionship, and good cheer are simply gone forever. Yet I must carry on quietly with an ever widening gap of emptiness in the tapestry of my days.

To compensate for this inevitable loss, I have learned to turn more and more to the wondrous companionship of God my Father, who has become ever so dear. I have learned to find profound fulfillment for the ever widening emptiness in the precious presence of Christ Himself, my closest Friend, my Savior, my inspiration, my very life. I have learned to rely implicitly on the comradeship of His gracious Spirit to guide me, to counsel me, to empower me to be bold and brave in the midst of so much sorrow.

To paraphrase 2 Timothy 1:7: "For God my Father has not given me the spirit of fear. Rather He has given me continually His own wondrous Spirit who bestows the power, the love, and the sound mind of Christ Himself, who enables me to carry on with courage."

This has not been written to impress the reader. Nor does it express any pretensions to piety. I make no claim to be a super-spiritual saint. Quite the opposite! I am a rough-hewn, rugged sort of mountain man who has found quiet companionship and rich consolation in the close company of the eternal One who never changes. He does not grow old or infirm. His enthusiasm and encouragement never diminish. His strength and endurance never fail. His goodwill and his good cheer are forever fresh and new every dawn.

And therein lies the source of my courage to carry on. Therein springs the secret fountain of unshakable faith to face the future without fear or foreboding. Therein resides the serenity to push on in an ever more lonely life. I have said it hundreds of times before; I say it again: "He is here. All is well!"

What I have just expressed about the realm of soul and spirit applies equally to the stern and inescapable attrition of our physical bodies. I am fully aware of the improved health and increasing life spans for seniors. The scientific community boasts much about the elderly living to well over a hundred years. All of this in sharp contrast to the rather brief lives of former generations.

But the golden years simply are not all gold!

We are not guaranteed immortality.

The passing of time takes its toll.

Physical stamina wanes. Energy ebbs away.

Bodies break down. Faculties become feeble.

We all make jokes about this sad attrition. We try to see the silver lining. With brave smiles we try to laugh it off. But in our moments alone it calls for courage to carry on.

Most of my life I have known only fragile health and marginal strength. Because I have lived so close to the "edge" for so long, death holds no great fear for me. In order to survive and to serve effectively, I have made every effort to live a disciplined life that would provide some measure of physical vitality.

Sound nutrition, ample exercise, sufficient rest, abundant fresh air and sunshine, drinking pure liquids, living in quiet contentment, enjoying a calm trust in God my Father have contributed to an extended life span. Many of my associates marvel at my capacity to still carry a fairly full workload into old age.

But physical vigor diminishes.

The old resilience to make a comeback is fading.

The will and the spirit remain strong but bone and blood, muscle and tendons, grow weary.

It calls for courage just to carry on!

So in what simple, steadfast way does one face this formidable, inexorable decline in vigor and vitality? It is Christ again who supplies us with the supreme secret. He exhorts us earnestly to live calmly in the limited context of this immediate moment, of this single day given as a gift to be cherished.

In other words, I need to make the most of this moment. I shall never, ever have it again. There is no guarantee whatever about tomorrow. I need to draw joy, contentment, peace, and delight from this day as He opens my awareness to all He shares with me.

For many years now I have called this way of life with Him, "Living with God in an attitude of gratitude." In giving Him my constant thanks He finds joy. He, in turn, pours benefits and bonuses upon me in great abundance. With those I find His courage to carry on!

CHAPTER TWENTY-ONE

Stillness, Solitude, Serenity

As a youngster I knew almost nothing about tight-knit, supportive family life. My earliest recollections are shot through with vivid, stabbing impressions of a small lad who felt he was a "bit of a bother" to others. I did not say "a bit of a brother." There is a world of difference between the two.

Somehow, in a strange way, I never felt I truly belonged to a family, a peer group, or any human community. It seemed I was a misfit, never truly accepted anywhere because of my rather wild and restless makeup.

For me growing up was not a joyous experience. It was a never-ending struggle to survive as one despised and rejected by others. Little marvel that by early manhood I had become very much a "lone wolf" who would not allow others to abuse me.

No one ever truly understood the fierce flames of inner independence that burned within my soul. It was simply assumed that I was starkly antisocial because I was a rough, tough frontier type who "did not fit."

All of which shaped the contours of my character well into midlife. During this period I really was difficult. I drove myself very hard. And I demanded much too much of others around me. I was an enigma to others, a grief to my family, and a stranger to God my Father.

Yet, wonder of wonders, in His mercy, compassion, grace, and patience, Christ saw and understood me as a wild and willful man. Steadily, surely, by His own gracious Spirit He persevered in drawing me to Himself. It took years and years for me to come to Him, to know Him, to trust Him, to learn to love Him.

Much of His transforming work took place in solitude, in stillness, in profound silence, but with calm serenity.

For this reason, an aspect of life that matters most to me are the times of utter stillness, quiet solitude, and gentle serenity when I commune with Christ Himself in profound intimacy. It takes time, effort, and disciplined determination to find solitude in our brash and busy world. But for me these quiet moments in company with my Father are among the most cherished in all of life.

I am not referring to anything supernatural or even mystical. Often in my books, even more so in my lectures, I have pointed out our profound need to get alone with God. It was most important in Christ's life when He was among us as a man. How much more so then for us! He is my hope!

For one thing, we need to be still and alone in the presence of our Father in order to gain His perspective on those things that matter most in life. Only He has the eternal, enduring view of an ever-changing earth scene. Only He can bring a calm serenity and sure stability into our shifting scenes. For only He endures ever the same. Only He understands all things from the beginning to end. Only He understands me. Only He brings enormous hope into life!

It is for these reasons I earnestly endeavor, each day, no matter how pressured I may be, to slip away alone to spend time with Him. These are precious, precious interludes. For in the stillness and in the solitude He refreshes my spirit, restores my soul, and reenergizes my body.

For me as a common, rough-cut man, there has been remarkable healing, help, and wholeness in His presence. It matters not how abrasive my world may be, no matter how abusive my contemporaries may seem, no matter how atrocious the circumstances of life may appear, each and every one becomes bearable under the touch of His life on mine. For He is my expectant hope!

In the stillness and serenity of His person I discover how He endured so much suffering at the hands of His antagonists. It is there I see why, though He was reviled, He did not revile His adversaries. It is there I begin to comprehend how He always took the high ground of generous and noble living. So it follows that, if in fact I share His life, I can prevail in peace and goodwill and confident hope.

In the solitude and stillness of these intimate moments with Him, an acute awareness of His power, His peace, and His very person pervades my entire being. I come away renewed and re-created, able to face the stress and strain of life with serenity.

This is the way in which He wants me to live.

He finds no pleasure in fickle conduct.

He is not amused by our foolish ways.

He expects us to live by faith and not in fear.

He wants us to know He is always here with hope.

How can we live according to His will if we rush along in hot pursuit of quick fixes and easy answers to our troubles? Many of them are of long duration. Difficult and demanding circumstances do not just go away. Some challenges will confront us for months and years.

So the only sure panacea for most problems in life as God's child is to have our Father's perspective. Once we begin to see things as He does, our difficulties diminish, not necessarily in scale but in seriousness. We begin to understand, even if only slightly, the bizarre behavior of others. This gives us some of His compassion toward them, and some of His ability to forgive and love them.

It is inevitable that profound, powerful changes will gradually take place when we spend time in stillness and serious communion with our Father. What matters most is that He finds joy by our humble devotion. He finds enormous pleasure in our interactions with Him and is sweetly satisfied to share Himself with His children.

Seven remarkable results flow from this precious, personal oneness between the Father and us. I conclude this book simply by stating these results.

(1) It is in stillness that Christ reveals Himself. I actually get to know Him firsthand. He is no longer a distant deity. He is present in personal encounters to impart His faith, His hope, His love to me.

I am not hearing about Him from a third party—a priest, a practitioner, or some other person. The Most High, by His Spirit, through His supernatural truth, speaks to my spirit in unmistakable inner convictions.

As John, the much beloved aged disciple, declared so adamantly in His remarkable letter to fellow Christians: We know, we know, we know Him! This theme is the heartbeat of his life with God. This pleases God!

(2) This quiet time together leads to a compelling love of enormous loyalty. I love simply because it is a sublime inner response to His love. Like begets like. I become like the One with whom I spend much time.

And our time together creates calm contentment between us. Bonds of love and loyalty, stronger than steel, bind us together. We become as one. This is a profound honor of eternal consequence, for it is in truth a foretaste of heaven.

Marvel of marvels is His love imparted to me by His Spirit that enables me to go out and live for Him, to comply with His commands in great goodwill, to quietly carry out His will with good cheer.

He is mine! I am His! Herein is my hope!

(3) In this intense intimacy, His faith becomes an integral force within my soul. I learn to trust Him in childlike confidence, not because someone else urges me to do so, but for the simple reason that He has reached out to touch my own soul. He has opened my darkened sight to see Him as He really is. He has drawn near to my searching spirit and fully satisfied my longing with His life.

Oh, I can only say in all earnestness, taste and see for yourself how good and gracious and generous He is. This is not self-delusion. It is not self-hypnosis. He is utterly faithful, totally trustworthy—so very different from all human associates.

I can trust Him and not be afraid. Oh, how this thrills Him! And how it stills my own soul in hope.

(4) In the quiet interaction there flows between us a deep current of pure delight. I have written an entire volume on this theme, *God Is My Delight.* But it needs to be reiterated here, for it is extremely precious and matters most between God my Father and me.

He, too, loves to delight in my companionship. He longs to have me linger in the sheer, uncomplicated joy of our mutual friendship. He is my bright hope!

This powerful connection is not some sort of spurious mysticism. It is the plain, potent compulsion of the serene joy He shares with me when I come to Him in honest humility but with abounding praise and thanks.

When I walk along the beach, as I follow the shoreline, it is impossible to suppress the pure praise that surges up within my spirit. I have to sing in quiet ecstasy. The gulls and the sandpipers rise on the sea wind to join in my jubilant joy. Sky and sea and shore all sing in unison. Hope springs anew in my spirit.

(5) In stillness I serenely abandon myself to God in gladness. Most surely I have said enough for anyone to realize that this is not asking too much! This is a reasonable and

appropriate action of my will in quiet response to all His mercy and loving-kindness.

He constantly surrounds me with His unending care. He enfolds me in His compassion. He forgives all my faults. He heals all my injuries. Why should I not just fling my whole being into His gentle, kind, wondrous care? Why hold back? Why delay?

He gives and gives and gives of His surprising life and bounties to anyone who offers Him open access to all they are and have. Our Father actually searches the earth for individuals who will literally abandon themselves to His care. He finds very few. But they are blessed in wondrous ways! They become strong in His faith, hope, and love.

(6) In the quiet times He comes bringing rest and repose to those who decide, by deliberate acts of their wills, to follow Christ calmly. At last their souls are serene and their spirits are still in His presence.

There is a remarkable life of rest in him.

The fret and friction of our feverish days are done.

The fears that haunted us are dispelled. His buoyant love and abundant life drive out our dark despair.

His glorious light banishes the darkness. We are free!

His presence sets us free from all fear. His power sets us free to follow Him gladly. His peace sets us free to live in peace, no matter what men may do! We live in quiet hope!

This is what it means to find rest of soul in Him.

And it is what brings enormous satisfaction to Him.

(7) In close communion with God, we become consecrated to Him. When our Father finds someone who desires to have an intimate relationship with Him, He sets that person apart as a special recipient of His grace and generosity.

This is reasonable and right. For most people actually keep God at arm's length. They close off large segments of their souls to Him. They exclude Him from their innermost being. They are reluctant to give up control of their choices. So He is not free to live and move and have His way with them. Consequently they cut themselves off from His benefits.

But the children of God who eagerly open up all of their life to Christ will discover He loves to come in and share every day with them. He revels in filling their lives with His own abundant life. Then suddenly they discover this life of consecration is not confining. It is actually a joyous adventure with Him!

This intimate sharing with His children satisfies Him in wondrous ways. He is pleased to pour out endless benefits on souls such as these.

And He, in turn, uses His people to enrich others, imparting hope and help and healing! This above all else really matters most! Can He say of me at the close of my brief sojourn here, "This is My child in whom I am well pleased"?